# Editorial

In 1975 the South African poet David Wright sent me a long poem by Julian Orde Abercrombie entitled 'The Conjurors'. The first of its thirty rhymed seven-line stanzas, charting the metamorphosis of a caterpillar from grub to chrysalis to imago, reads,

> This crusty July, blackfly
>     And other small, moist flies –
>         Whiskers so thin
>         They are not felt on skin –
> Liking a dry July
>     Interrupted the performance
>     Of the opening of some flowers.

This poem featured in *Poetry Nation* VI (1976). Two issues earlier we published Wright's elegy to Orde, evoking their long friendship. It refused to abandon the present tense. Shared friendships, art, intimacy, the Blitz, illuminate its lines:

> The summer of pilotless planes,
> Of searchlit nights and soft,
> When once upon a scare
> Together we ran out
>
> Into the naked garden
> High over Archway, and
> The warm leaves of laurel
> Trembled in no wind.

Vicki Beatson, heir of the Wright papers, and James Keery, well known to readers of *PN Review*, are giving shape to the correspondence of David Wright. Orde and Wright come alive. The elegiac stanzas and the letters are close up in a new age of pilotless planes and invasive events.

> And there remains a large room full of flowers
>     Imaged on canvases, the real ones still in the garden,
> And books and objects I've known for thirty years.
>     Unknown to me I am taking a final leave of them
>
> And the woman no longer young but more beautiful
>     Than the young girl had been, who held all these together.
> Yet that web woven over so long shall not unravel,
>     Though the lives and bonds disperse like the furniture
>
> To disassociation. Eternity, when one thinks of it,
>     Exists in what has been, there residing. [...]

Orde appeared again in *PN Review* 2 (1978) with a selection of fifteen poems made by Wright and accompanied by a memoir that regrets he had not seen, appreciated and promoted the later work. His advocacy in 1978 was an act of restitution. He sent the poems to several editors. One of them was me.

His elegy prepared the ground, a powerful set of formal memory fragments which brought the 'Jill of all trades' to life. 'The Conjurors' followed the elegy a few months later. I took to it in the way I came to love Marianne Moore's 'The Steeplejack' and Elizabeth Bishop's obliquely confessional 'Over 2000 Illustrations and a Complete Concordance'. Then Wright sent a selection from the typescript Orde's daughter assembled after her death. (Geoffrey Hill, in a private letter to him, remarked, 'At the risk of being misunderstood, I'd say someone as good as this had a duty to herself to be consistently better.')

We ran our long selection of her poems, then Wright sent me the typescript itself.

For some reason I shilly-shallied. I did not rise to the challenge. But I was haunted. By the time I wanted to revisit the poems, Wright had died, the script could not be found. I was dogged by my indecision (which was a kind of decision). The book hadn't gone elsewhere: it had gone.

Wright had a substantial impact on Carcanet and *PN Review* in their early years. Vicki Beatson in 2012 contacted me about Wright's letters, with the proposal that we consider them for publication. They opened a window on many – most – of my favourite mid-twentieth-century poets including Sisson, Graham, Barker, Singer, as well as painters and other artists. James Keery, who edited the Carcanet anthology *Apocalypse*, began collaborating with Vicki. Was it possible that they might find, or reconstruct, the Orde collection? The degree of my original interest was clear from Wright's letters: he even told Orde's daughter in the 1970s that I had said I would publish.

In the long-term event, he was not wrong. Five decades later the book is scheduled to appear in September under the title *Conjurors*. Editing is sometimes a geologically slow process: the fates of Charlotte Mew, Stevie Smith, Rosemary Tonks, Miles Burrows, E.J. Scovell, Brigit Pegeen Kelly and many others are evidence that poetry publishing is not always about today and tomorrow. Some illuminating, illuminated tomorrows are to be found among all our yesterdays. Reading James Keery's *Apocalypse* anthology, the twentieth century reconfigures itself. As David Wright reflects in his *PNR* Orde memoir:

> The neo-romanticism of the 1940s infected nearly the whole generation that was born around the Great War in time for the next. Everybody had it, like measles; even those who are not now thought of as neo-romantics – Keith Douglas, Philip Larkin, Norman MacCaig for example – caught the infection to begin with. Few recovered; but I think that those who did, eventually wrote the better for that inoculation. The fever (for it was more of a malady than a fashion) was I think due to the impact of the sprung verse of Hopkins (whose *Wreck of the Deutschland* opened Michael Roberts's influential *Faber Book of Modern Verse* in 1936), and to the almost coincident publication of *Finnegans Wake* and Yeats's last poems with the outbreak of a long-expected war; also to the near-mesmeric influence of two contemporary exploiters of language, George Barker and Dylan Thomas, whose poems caught the apocalyptic feel of the times and offered our generation a different fare to the politico-sociological gruel served by their immediate predecessors [...] [T]he poems of Julian's that I knew were nearly all 'forties' poems, many of them smudged by the surreal imagery of the period. Yet the best now seem to me to be better than most of the stuff that appeared in the magazines and slim volumes of those days, and of these days, come to think of it.

It's hard for me to imagine the middle of the twentieth century now without Julian Orde Abercrombie. It's my extraordinary good luck to publish her thanks to James Keery's and Vicki Beatson's archaeology, at last honouring a promise not quite made by *PN Review* in its early years. Sometimes editors can serve the whirligig of time, to the benefit of readers for whom poetry is never a settled canon. The past, even the recent past, is at least as rich in resource and surprise as the present.

# Letters to the Editor

### Topless feminists running amok

*Vona Groarke writes:* Much as I love the idea of topless feminists running amok around County Tipperary, the 'Femen' cited in my book, *Woman of Winter* (reviewed by Gwyneth Lewis in *PN Review* 276), is, in fact, the Plain of Femen, from which arises Sliabh na mBan, (which translates from Irish as 'Mountain of the Women', and is probably better known to folk singers as 'Slievenamon').

That said, I'm sure the locals would be only too delighted to offer a hospitable (if rather rainy) and semantically apt base to the Ukrainian activist group of the same name.

### Political Content, and Discontent

*Dave Wynne-Jones writes:* I'd like to commend Andrew Hadfield on the hard-hitting opening paragraphs of his review of John Sutherland's *Triggered Literature* and indeed the analysis forming the body of that review, 'Welcome to the Culture Wars'. However, the culture wars he describes are more widely located than the campuses and literary targets that he and his subject focus on in *PNR* 275. In the same edition, Isabel Galleymore examines the effects of a shared imagery on environmental thinking, almost a displacement activity, and Horatio Morpurgo, writing on Lipkin, draws our attention to the way 'the role of literary magazines in supporting the structure of truthfulness as a language is subjected to immense distorting pressures'. In an article in which he manages to air his views on the war in Ukraine, Morpurgo never once mentions the roles of NATO and the US in a conflict that has been going on since 2014. With intentional irony on page 4 of edition 274, *PNR* noted the censorship of an anti-Zionist Jewish poet and his reviewer practised by Chicago's *Poetry* magazine, whilst also commenting on the 'Funding Crisis' which undoubtedly bears some responsibility for less obvious editorial decisions in the UK, as Arts Council funding shrinks and magazines find that they risk closure if readers cancel subscriptions because of controversial content.

An eco-poet and academic who has been published for decades described to me how a submission to a particular magazine was systematically filleted of its political content before publication. Last year's Cheltenham festival promised better with an eco-poetry event featuring Ruth Padel and Jonathan Porritt, but the shared poems said little beyond 'isn't nature wonderful!' whilst in follow-up discussion, satire was deemed to have become the province of social media and stand-up comedy, rather than of poetry. And where is the political poetry that we might have expected to emerge from the salutary experience of Covid?

Since 7 October we have seen an immense mobilisation of establishment power to censor and cancel views that are not in line with a sponsored narrative, comparable only to the anti-Corbyn mobilisation in this country in the years leading up to the 2019 election. Regarding campuses, we have seen McCarthyite interrogations and resignations of the heads of prestigious US universities. German authorities have axed funding to organisations, withdrawn literary prizes and cancelled events not only for Palestinians but also for Jewish artists and writers who have condemned the actions of Israel in Gaza.

At a time when the establishment has never been more concerned to maintain its control over the narrative expressed in the mainstream media, the suppression of dissident views can have profound and insidious effects, not least on poetry. Anne Boyer's resignation as the Poetry editor of the *New York Times* draws attention to the effect on language of such suppression: 'I can't write about poetry amidst the "reasonable" tones of those who aim to acclimatize us to this unreasonable suffering. No more ghoulish euphemisms. No more verbally sanitized hellscapes. No more warmongering lies.... If this resignation leaves a hole in the news the size of poetry, then that is the true shape of the present.' Cinnamon Press has rushed into print with Omar Sabbagh's *RIP*, but, even though some Palestinian poets are being featured online, where else is the political poetry about the catastrophe in Gaza?

Within my workshop group, poets seem to be struggling with the enormity of what is happening, but the performance poetry circuit could have been expected to have more resilience and nimbleness in its responses. Unfortunately, there seems to have been a marked lack of engagement there too. As we saw post-Covid, most performers have returned to the same old mixture of identity politics, adolescent angst and comedy rhymes. One poet suggested to me that the effect was similar to what he'd experienced growing up in his minority ethnic community when people 'kept their heads down', not wanting to draw attention to themselves because of the unpredictability of the responses they might receive. It's unfortunate that so often attempts to write about Gaza draw accusations of antisemitism, despite anti-Zionism having recently been established by legal precedent as a philosophical belief protected under the 2010 Equalities Act in the UK.

Understandably, writers are likely to avoid getting drawn into such a potentially damaging arena, but the effects on poetry and society can be equally harmful. For the individual, an inability to validate their thoughts and feelings in what they read and hear can result in repression and associated cognitive dissonance. For the poet, a turning away from controversial subjects can lead to a rigorously subjective, self-centred focus that discourages engagement with larger and wider issues. For society, dissent 'goes underground', government becomes less responsive to those it governs (as we have seen in this country with legislation to curtail the right to strike or peacefully protest) and views are increasingly polarised. Ahead of her review, published on 25 March, Dame Sara Khan, the Government's independent social cohesion adviser, has revealed that polling for her report found that more than 75 percent of the public feel they have to refrain from speaking their mind.

In a culture war it's not so much a question of taking sides but of shaping a supportive community in which conflicting views can be expressed and heard, in an effort to reach a better understanding (even agreement, as we discovered in Northern Ireland). Peace negotiations need to recognise both parties. Poets may no longer be the 'unacknowledged legislators of the world', but poetry still has a part to play in 'the creative faculty to imagine that which we know'. Given the current economic and political pressures on the academic and the publishing worlds, it's a moot point whether they can rise to the occasion.

Giving credit where it's due...

*Anthony Barnett writes:* Further to 'AI and Poetry' by Robert Griffiths (*PNR* 276) there's more than one kind of AI: For example, the review *Snow lit rev* is edited by A(nthony Barnett) and I(an Brinton) and published by A(llardyce) I(ntelligence).

Thank you, AI.

# News and Notes

---

**Marjorie Perloff** • *James Campbell writes:* Marjorie Perloff, who has died aged ninety-two, was an unrelenting champion of the New, in literature, in art, and most other things. When it came to aesthetic appreciation, however, she was a defender of traditional critical values and a sworn foe of the modern – but not Modernist – trend of identity approval. Marjorie had just turned seventy when I invited her to write for the *TLS*. I did so after reading her letter to the editor of the *London Review of Books*, critical of remarks in its symposium on the attacks of September 11, 2001. She proceeded to write one *TLS* review after another, fuelled by close reading, on subjects ranging from D.H. Lawrence to Concrete Poetry, Hart Crane to Tom Raworth. To borrow a term from popular music, Marjorie's reviews had 'attack'. She was a generous critic, though never afraid to go on the attack in the more usual sense.

In her final decade, Marjorie published several books, among them a study of writers of the Austrian diaspora (*Edge of Irony*), a two-volume collection of her reviews (*Circling the Canon*), and her final and most surprising success, a translation of Ludwig Wittgenstein's *Private Notebooks: 1914–1916*, warmly received on publication in 2022. Her first book, *Frank O'Hara: Poet among the Painters* (1977), was the earliest study of the poet.

She was a vigorous correspondent – not lower-case jottings, but opinionated letters (though the medium was email), often containing stories about the good and the great of American poetry. Knowing my interest in the Black Mountain poets, she recalled how, in 1976, she organized a series of readings near her home in Los Angeles with Edward Dorn and Robert Duncan, among others. 'Dorn turned out to be great company and interesting, but Duncan was impossible. He was on the wagon (so he said), until he started drinking everything and anything he found in the bar, talking non stop about Baudelaire, theosophy – anything. There was something so pre-Raphaelite about him that made me, as a Modernist, nervous.'

She left Austria in 1938 at the age of six. Her memoir, *The Vienna Paradox*, recounted the travails of family upheaval as the Nazi threat rose. Whenever she found herself at the 30th Street Station in Philadelphia, Marjorie wrote, 'or Euston Station in London or the Gare du Nord in Paris, I feel unaccountably sad'. She attributed this 'train phobia' to the night of 13 March 1938, 'the night I left Vienna for Zurich on the train'.

Marjorie's directness was part of her charm. When I was in Los Angeles in 2008, on commission from the *Guardian* to profile Gore Vidal, she picked me up at the (I thought) pleasant hotel where I was staying in Hollywood. Stepping inside for a moment, she looked around and said, 'Can't the *Guardian* do better than this?' After lunch at the Beverley Hills Hotel, she drove me to her house in Pacific Palisades, a splendid place in a natural dip, surrounded by trees. 'And this is the Pound room', Marjorie said, gesturing towards book-lined walls.

In my last email, sent a few days before she died, in the knowledge that the end was imminent, I wrote: 'I loved working with you as editor to writer. I used to say, "When a book has been reviewed by Marjorie, *it knows it has been reviewed.*"'

**Alan Brownjohn** • *Maren Meinhardt writes:* The poet Alan Brownjohn died on 23 February in London at the age of ninety-two. He was the poetry editor of the *New Statesman* (1968–74), chaired the Poetry Society (1982–8), and worked as the poetry critic for the *Sunday Times* for more than two decades.

Influenced by the poets of the Movement, and a member of The Group clustered around Philip Hobsbaum, he once said of his work, 'I write nothing without hoping it might make the world one grain better – a pompous statement which, I suppose, makes me a moralist as a writer, a humanist one.' This social engagement was not confined to his writing: he contested the seat of Richmond for the Labour Party (unsuccessfully), campaigned for nuclear disarmament, and backed the republication of James Kirkup's poem 'The Love That Dares To Speak Its Name', which had been found to be blasphemous in a private prosecution brought by Mary Whitehouse.

Brownjohn loved cats – 'A Bad Cat Poem' is, ostensibly, about a couple's failure to teach a cat how to use a cat flap. It was an expression, perhaps, of his non-conformist leanings that his own cat should have been a Manx cat. The collection *Ludbrooke & Others* appeared in 2010, when Brownjohn was in his seventies, and is perhaps the culmination of the best tendencies in his work. Widely admired, it concerns the progress of Ludbrooke in love, rejection and the hope – against experience – of worldly success and, perhaps even more importantly, of cutting a dash. Most of the sonnets are made up of thirteen lines. As Kit Wright put it in the eulogy on his friend delivered at the funeral, they are like cats without a tail.

Brownjohn's unorthodox tendencies carried over into the sartorial realm. In later years, he developed a fondness for wearing suits in a range of alarming pastel shades, of which I remember, in particular, the lilac and the pink. This made him easy to spot at literary parties, where he was a fixture, and where his gently-amused, friendly presence will be missed.

**The kitchen of our childhood** • *Patrick McGuinness writes:* The poet Guy Goffette died in Namur on 28 March at the age of seventy-six. Born in Jamoigne, in the Belgian Lorraine in 1947, he was brought up in a working-class rural family near three borders: Belgium, France and Luxembourg. After his studies at the Ecole normale in Arlon, where he was inspired to write poetry by his tutor, Vital Lahaye, he became a schoolteacher in Rouvroy. In 1969 he published his first volume of poems, *Quotidien rouge*, and began what would become a lifelong association with what is called, in French, 'l'édition'. He began editing, in 1980, the literary review *Triangle*, and took on L'Apprentypographe, a limited edition press publishing fine books on fine paper, which Goffette himself typeset.

The book that brought him to the notice of the French literary establishment was *Eloge pour une cuisine de Province*, which appeared in 1988 from Champ Vallon and won him the Prix Mallarmé. His next book, *La Vie promise*, appeared in 1991 from Gallimard, where, after giving up school-teaching, he became an editor and a member of the editorial board. He was a prolific poet, producing more than a dozen volumes, but he also wrote livres d'artistes, pamphlets and several volumes of prose,

including, in 1996, his *Verlaine d'ardoise et de pluie*, a short and haunting experiment in biographical writing, a novel about Bonnard, and, in 2013, a lightly fictionalised autobiographical novel about his brutal, taciturn father, *Geronimo a mal au dos*, a sequel to his earlier *Un été autour du cou* (2001).

Goffette's work is known for its lyricism and its virtuosic but never forced mastery of a range of tones and modes as well as verse forms. Like Verlaine, he believed that poetry must remain faithful to the idea of voice, and there is a quality of *spokenness* to all his work, however learned or allusive, which gives it a unique warmth. Yves Bonnefoy wrote of him:

> Goffette is an heir to Verlaine. A poet who very courageously has decided to remain faithful to his own personal life, in its humblest moments. He keeps things simple, he is marvellously able to capture the emotions and desires common to us all. Goffette is without question one of the best poets of the present moment in France.

A popular and approachable poet, he was also, in his way, a 'poet's poet', despite steering clear of cliques and *cénacles*. Among the many prizes he won, of particular note are the Grand prix de poésie de l'Académie francaise, the Prix Goncourt de la poésie and the Prix Max-Jacob in France, and the Prix Victor-Rossel and the Prix Félix-Denayer in Belgium.

Goffette thought of himself as always *en partance*, about to leave, and *en lisière*, on the margins. In 2020 he published *Pain perdu*, a volume in which – after a stroke and during Covid, and unable to write new poems – he revisited and retouched old drafts and aborted versions of old poems, and turned them into a book. The title – 'French Toast' would be the name in English – refers to stale bread that is dipped in egg, cooked and served with sugar as a treat. In a moving interview for TV Lux, Goffette spoke of how he returned to these poems at a time of exhaustion and illness, when he thought he had nothing left 'in the kitchen cupboard', and how, with a bit of invention and a few extra ingredients (time being one of them) he made new dishes. It would have been a symbolic and fitting last volume, but his next book, *Paris à ma porte*, appeared in 2023. Also in 2023, Éditions Labor in Belgium published a substantial Selected Poems under the title *L'Oiseau de craie*.

'We all one day return to the kitchen of our childhood', wrote Goffette. When he retired from Gallimard and came back to live in Belgium, in the Gaume of his childhood, he bought a house in the small town of Lacuisine. It is uncannily fitting for a poet who bridged the distance between the country and the city, the French metropolis and the Belgian *terroir*, the kitchen and the *salon*.

**The Open Text** • The death at the age of eighty-two of the poet Lyn Hejinian was announced in late March. Her revolutionary moment began in the 1960s when, as writer, publisher and university teacher, she was a central figure in the development of the Language Poetry Movement, initially a challenge to received conventions, in due course itself a convention.

Its anti-confessional polemic, tilting against the 'confessional' poetic perspectives of Robert Lowell and John

Berryman, among others, produced a wealth of theoretical and creative work. The first person became a vexed zone for the poet to occupy. Language writing developed in San Francisco and New York City and featured poets including Rae Armantrout, Carla Harryman, Ron Silliman and Charles Bernstein. Hejinian set up Tuumba Press around a manual letterpress machine to showcase Language writing. Gertrude Stein was a chief influence, and on the theoretical side Roland Barthes. The poems featured were, in Bernstein's words, 'as much about how they make meaning as what they mean'. 'Often the poems evaded any direct message in favour of an attention to the language of the poem and its sonic rhythms.'

Under the influence of the anti-Vietnam war, civil rights and feminist movements, Hejinian and other poets advocated writing 'that allows for a multiplicity of points of view and meanings', as though this was something entirely new. Her essay 'The Rejection of Closure' (1983) was a key text for these poets. 'The open text is one which both acknowledges the vastness of the world and is formally differentiating. It is form that provides an opening.' In rejecting closure, 'the writer relinquishes total control and challenges authority as a principle and control as a motive'. Language writing 'resists the cultural tendencies that seek to identify and fix material and turn it into a product; that is, it resists reduction and commodification'.

Hejinian liked being an insider/outsider, a 'maverick': 'We attended and participated in poetry readings that took place two or three or sometimes four times a week, talked until late at night at bars, launched literary journals, hosted radio shows, curated readings and lecture series', she declared in 2020. 'We had very little respect for official academia, which, in turn, had very little respect for us.' Until it did, and it assimilated the threat that Language writing had seemed to pose. A selection of her essays was published by University of California Press and, while not widely read, her example and and her theory are widely referenced.

**Copyright and AI** • The Artificial Intelligence (AI) Act was adopted with a large majority by the European Parliament on Wednesday 13 March. In California, a US district judge largely sided with OpenAI, dismissing the majority of claims raised by authors alleging that large language models powering ChatGPT were illegally trained on pirated copies of their books, without their permission.

The European legislation proposes basic obligations on the AI firms in the field of copyright. General purpose AI (such as generative AI) is expected to respect copyright law and formally articulate policies to ensure transparency. 'The EU now has rules that will be a model for the rest of the world. The AI Act recalls basic but fundamental principles that AI companies must respect. They must respect EU copyright law and actively ensure that they do, even if the AI was trained outside of Europe. They will finally have to be transparent on the data used to train their AI, which, to their own admission, relies on the use of copyright protected content.'

The California judge for her part decided that there was insufficient evidence to prove the case, rejecting

most ChatGPT copyright claims from book authors. The judge resolved that the distinguished authors behind three separate lawsuits had 'failed to provide evidence supporting any of their claims except for direct copyright infringement', surely a sufficient 'except' to cast the judgement in doubt. The judge importantly and tendentiously approved OpenAI's claim that when authors alleged that 'every' ChatGPT output 'is an infringing derivative work', their case was 'insufficient' to sustain an allegation of 'vicarious infringement, which requires evidence that ChatGPT outputs are "substantially similar" or "similar at all" to authors' books'. The absence of 'factual' evidence weakened the authors' case.

Positioning itself for the next general election, the Publisher's Association declared that the value of the publishing sector in the UK was £11 billion to the economy. With greater government backing, this value could increase by 50 percent by 2033. The report specifies ten areas for development which include delivering 'AI opportunities for the whole economy'. The numbers are impressive:

- **£11 billion** – contribution of UK publishing sector to the UK economy overall
- **84,000** – number of jobs supported by UK publishing in 2024, which is predicted to grow by **43,000** by 2033
- **£6.5 billion** – gross value added of publishing exports
- **20 percent** – growth in international demand for UK publishing by 2033

The Publishers' Association has imprinted these statistics on the minds of government and opposition cultural spokespersons.

**Yale Young Poet** • In February, Lohn Liles won the 2024 Yale Younger Poets award, a competition that brings attention to America's promising new poets. Liles is a poet and science writer of 'dense, sonically gorgeous studies' of the natural world and of the human heart, described as both 'scientifically grounded and emotionally engaged'. Liles's collection is entitled *Bees, and after*. The selector was Rae Armantrout. *Bees, and after* will be published by Yale University Press in April 2025.

It is Armantrout's fourth selection as official selector. The press release says that 'Liles's work is predicated on academic and archival research – "a writing process that necessitates achieving an organic/animal understanding of the present surviving phenomenon". Aiming to establish a new interdisciplinary space between the arts and sciences, Liles holds to a self-established canon where the scientific must remain true.' He lives in Fort Bragg, California, where 'he writes and works as the head naturalist at the Pacific Environmental Education Center, a nonprofit organization that provides standards-based, residential marine environmental education programs to schools throughout northern California.'

**Incisive ideas and necessary questions** • *Guernica*, a little, distinguished online literary journal, published, and then retracted, a personal essay about coexistence and war in the Middle East by an Israeli writer, leading to resignations by volunteer staff who objected to its publication. The website includes the unambiguous statement, 'Guernica *regrets having published this piece, and has retracted it. A more fulsome explanation will follow.*'

The essay by Joanna Chen was entitled 'From the Edges of a Broken World'. Chen is a translator of Hebrew and Arabic poetry and prose. She had written about her experiences trying to bridge the divide with Palestinians, including by volunteering to drive Palestinian children from the West Bank to receive care at Israeli hospitals, and how her efforts to find common ground faltered after Hamas's attack of 7 October and Israel's subsequent attacks on Gaza. Among the resignations was that of the former co-publisher, Madhuri Sastry, who said that the essay 'attempts to soften the violence of colonialism and genocide'. Chen responded in an email that she felt her critics had misunderstood 'the meaning of my essay, which is about holding on to empathy when there is no human decency in sight. It is about the willingness to listen, and the idea that remaining deaf to voices other than your own won't bring the solution.' Chen added that she had worked on the essay – her second for *Guernica* – with the magazine's editor in chief and publisher, Jina Moore Ngarambe. Over emails and in a one-hour phone conversation, Chen said, 'I was offered the distinct impression my essay was appreciated. I was given no indication that the editorial staff was not onboard.' Ngarambe, who in 2017 and 2018 worked at the *New York Times* as its East Africa bureau chief, did not reply to requests for comment on Monday and Tuesday.

Summer Lopez, the 'chief of free expression programs at PEN America', said 'a writer's published work should not be yanked from circulation because it sparks public outcry or sharp disagreement. The pressures on U.S. cultural institutions in this moment are immense. Those with a mission to foster discourse should do so by safeguarding the freedom to write, read, imagine and tell stories.' *Guernica* describes its mission to be 'a home for incisive ideas and necessary questions'.

# Reports

## Fragments on Fragments

### Letter from a Northern Town

#### ANTHONY VAHNI CAPILDEO

Green glass lines up on the edge of the kitchen sink. The ridged bottles were poison bottles, my poet-housemate Clare Shaw. cheerfully tells me. Perfumes, poisons and pharmaceuticals: so often, these are interchangeable. Absinthe, the Green Fairy, intoxicant beloved of decadent poets, is a potent neurotoxin. The chemical name for this bitterness: thujone. Absinthe is derived from wormwood, an artemisia. Southernwood, a silvery-blue wormwood, intermixed with tall English lavender in planting, can be part of a traditional herbaceous border. Certainly, dried and hung in wardrobes, they help to keep off insects. Many familiar plants of humble growth also deter insects, but are of greater sweetness, which, chemically, arises from coumarin. Some of the bottles remain stoppered. Did they contain spirits? Some retain a sticky residue.

Clare has been mudlarking. You will know the activity: picking up bits of things from the edge of a river or sea – what my great-aunt, who told me off for 'gardening' as a child, might have condemned as 'playing in the dirt'. Cutting up materials or finding fragments and sticking them together is one, brilliantly defiant way of making something new, in our age of momentous rubbish. Mudlarking, however, is less papery than collage poetics. Although the activity is as old as our curious, liminal species, the word 'mudlark' is recorded as a noun only as recently as the eighteenth century, when (apparently) boys and men (or at least the activity has been masculinized in the interpretation of records) scavenged for items, in that age of terrible globalization. Britain was sending out new monsters to play on the deep. Scraps retrievable from where ships sailed or boats ventured, or foundered, became treasures in the practice of survival. Mudlarking, gendered muscly, was intent, intense, and linked to bare living as well as bringing the weird happiness of discovery, collection, the miniature. 'Mudlark' may be a play on 'skylark'. It is no accident that the revolutionary but elevated Shelleyan poetics of an empyrean perspective nowadays share space and value with the down-to-earth poetics of grubbing about in soil for the beauty of the left-behind, the recovered and the broken.

Each item that Clare rinses swiftly but thoroughly winks with the hint of a whole life, and way of life, that passed by in the local river, and in the river of time. Each fragment is a portal, a riddle. Clare laughs off any notion of making something – making some *thing* – say, a mosaic – from the fragments. Each is complete in itself. I can't help thinking of fragmented forms of poetry, or indeed prose poem sequences, and the tendency to read them as if they hang together; as if their intensely intentionally crafted shapes are fractured, demanding imaginative glue; as if we are invited to be fixers or Platonists, and to restore, or reach up to, some lost or implied form. Of course, there is poetry that insists on fracture. What about contentment with the fragment? As a poet, standing by the kitchen sink with Clare., I am aware of a kind of tidalectic movement within me; I want things to be themselves, and I want things to add up. My poor eyesight is a help. I hold – *not* a piece of a broken tea service – a glossy, blue-on-white image with water-softened curves – and think I discern part of a viol's body. A consort of music bows into hearing. I photograph it, to remember; and the image is re-membered. The camera reveals that it depicts a smiling cherub, not a musical instrument. Whether Venus's boy or a good angel, the bit of a thing returns my imagination to harmony... Is there no escaping a post-Romantic temptation to poetic perfection?

The poetics of working from mudlarked fragments felt heavenly, childlike: being allowed to love a detail without having to make sense or make a big deal... without having to write a report, or a novel; being able to love a part as a whole, without shattering, or forgetting, or even knowing, the whole that has yielded the part. Mudlarking sorts well with the unresolvable contradictions that belong with poetry, arising from syntax, breath, line break, ambiguity. Handling the new, river-curved objects that have arisen from old, fired curved vessels recommits me to the and/both that is a challenge in our age of fake news, that makes and inflames false divisions. As reader, writer, tangible creature, we can inherit the passion of Laura Mulvey and feminist critics of the violent dismemberment of feminized bodies in visual and other art... made for grabbing, boobily boobing, 'woman' never synonymous with an entire, ensouled, autonomous being. Rejection of the fragment after forced fragmentation. We can appreciate, too, the erotics of focusing on the tiny areas of a lover's body. David Plante, for example, is one of many authors writing beautifully of the unease and marvel of cis male homosexual encounters in our still-repressive society: at last, the lover can dwell on the detail of what he loves and wants, rather than denying its desirability. Adoration of the fragment after forced invisibilization.

In Virginia Woolf's *The Waves*, a polyvocal novel which would repay a tidalectic reading that is outwith the scope of this essay, the character Louis is often thought to have been based partly on T.S. Eliot. T.S. Eliot's *The Waste Land* is a mudlarked poem par excellence, a heap of broken images treated with excruciating care after the First World War leaves western civilization seeing itself as all washed up. Woolf's Louis needs only one poem throughout his life. He repeats it to himself in fragments throughout the novel... the Middle English lyric sometimes known as 'Westron Wynde', where rainfall makes the speaker long to be in bed with their absent love. His leitmotif sings of a missing other half. To read Louis this way is to have fragmented the Tom Eliot who was Virginia Woolf's friend. He brought her jazz records to listen to, while he taught her to dance the Chicken Strut. Despite the poetics of jazz being treated eloquently by writers including Ralph Ellison (easily available in the essay collection *Shadow and Act*), modernism tends to be broken off from its Black and musical aspects. These are sharp breaks, an impediment to artful handling. A properly tidalectic approach would trace the correspondence between T.S. Eliot and the innovative Guyanese poet A.J. Seymour. I keep saying this – not to recover a whole, but to inspire more mudlarking; letters are no more than pieces of literature, and lives.

A.J. Seymour's land of many rivers, Guyana, is also the birthplace of Martin Carter. Carter's lines are the *Westron Wyndes* to my Louis-life. They are refrains. In the everythingness that part drowns us, part tosses us hard onto humbling shores, different lines tumble out of memory. I am grateful to pick them up. In 'Till I Collect', contemplating the Atlantic Ocean, Carter's speaker hesitates. Unlike the fisherman, he dares not plunge his hand too far

lest only sand and shells I bring to air
lest only bones I resurrect to light.

I used to read this as the horror of ancestors and kinfolk being reduced to nameless bones; the Atlantic as the place where our common history went to die. It would be impossible for the poet to refashion individual skeletons from what was dredged up; or to recognize family; or to demand remembrance.

Writing now at Eastertide, and in the aftermath of a windstorm that saw trees falling on houses in my city this Scottish springtime, I read Carter as saying that the poet is no god. Of course, he will mudlark for bones – we can't resist and also, in another sense, we can only resist. Yet whatever life his words give, it is an afterlife. Poetry has no power to put flesh on actual fragments; cannot make them rise, walk and speak. Death pre-fragments Carter's poetic world, just as it did Eliot's, though hardly with the same poppy field vision applied to the ocean. I read Carter as reminding us that resurrection is different from revival. Lazarus was brought back from the dead – revived – which meant that he would run a course of life, ending in death again, like a normal mortal. Resurrection, on the other hand, raises our fragments made whole to eternal life. What would this mean for the poetics of memorialization, or of vivid consciousness? How can the statues of slavers be preserved, while Palestinian voices are censored as 'political' for singing in the darkest of times, when the bodies of children are under rubble? Whose is poetry? What images are allowed, or lovable? How can we look up?

# Set 4: Mondo de Melankolio

## TRANSLATED BY JOHN GALLAS

1

*Older and*          *Hjálmar Jónsson (1796–1875)/Iceland*

Age forbids me now to trick
the land with flowers of summer rhyme.
The stiff and hel-cold hand is sick
And eighty-odd is too much time.

2

*Apple*          *Manuel Bandeira (1886–1968)/Brazil*

From here you look like a puckered breast
from there a buttoned belly
where still the birth-cord stalks

Red as love divine

Inside you tiny seeds
tick with infinite
and monstrous life

And you sit so simply
by my knife, fork and spoon
in this shabby hotel room.

3

*High mountains: tick...*          *Anon/probably eighth-century Japan*

High mountains: tick.
The sea: tick.
Mountains go on being mountains,
indisputably mattering:
the other goes on being the sea,
and is unlikely to turn into anything else.
But people ah people
are rather unreliably *floral:*
quickly come, soon tattered, and *poof!* gone.

4

*Light leaving a small harbour*          *Chairil Anwar (1922–49)/Indonesia*

No glow of promises this time –
among the warehouses, woodhouses, rig-masts'
sad stutter. A beached bumboat, sealess ship,
prows at the dark, tugging, burring.

Thin rain and lightleaving. An eagle pitches,
flaps in dark thoughts, and out, coolly, away –
out to other love. Still. Still. Now,
coast and sky shut down with the waves.

Nothing. Only me. Walking,
looking for elsewhere, promises taken,
promises lost: giving them up, here,
on Beach No.4, the last gag of poison.

*Dawn*        *Hans Davidsohn (Jakob van Hoddis) (1887–1942) Jewish/German*

And so we traipse home, anxious and old –
(End of our cheery night-out). The sky,
Up past the streetlights, glowers and glimmers,
Blue and cold, with a big bully's eye.

The long streets squirm, leaden and blained,
And Dawn pokes us homewards, cringing and grey,
With redcold fingers, before it lets loose
Another compulsory, glorious day.

# Freedom Square

## RODERICK MENGHAM

There is a small, square badge that rests on a narrow shelf at the base of a wooden lectern in my room. I pick up and inspect this badge every time I use the lectern. The inspection is brief and unseeing, but the physical act of taking the square of metal and laying it in the palm of my hand is an important ritual. My fingers close around a talisman whose visual details I conjure up at will. A map of the country, or rather its silhouette, is superimposed on the national flag. At the centre of this empty vessel, this cartographic *terra nullius*, is the handwritten slogan of the people's liberation movement and the printed name of the place of issue. The same design could be found from one end of the country to the other, but always with the local name taking pride of place, a synecdoche of the nation, the part accepting responsibility for the whole.

The design of the slogan, a careful replica of rapid, freehand mark-making, has the urgent, defiant, improvisatory abandon of a graffito. Its style as contagious as its message, it would appear everywhere without warning at the height of the rebellion, materializing suddenly when no one was looking, as if appearing from the interior of buildings themselves, emerging under force, under pressure from the deep interior of history, rewriting itself with different words. How often do we see these messages come and go – and how often do we misread them, forget them, or put them out of mind?

Long ago in this very town, the famous astronomer who reimagined the laws by which all lives are governed inscribed them in the very fabric of this building, which is now called The Astronomer's House. Its three levels were dedicated to the principle of circulation in the three spheres of money, blood and the planets. It was circulation that maintained the health of society, the body and the unfixed stars, although the same motion would endanger the health of all three systems if any impurities should be introduced.

In the fog-deadened twilight, mechanical diggers burrow deep in the courtyards of ancient apartment buildings whose lamps flicker and go out. The drivers turn round in spilling gusts of night mist to spit their loads onto loose cobbles and frozen tram lines. They are slowly raising a barricade, in what used to be the Old Town Square. It had always housed a community that followed the old beliefs. But the members of this community were told they would have to move out while adjustments were made to prepare for the new living arrangements that would improve everyone's lives.

And so the residents were systematically evicted, even though no changes were made and no one arrived to take their place. As their last act, on the verge of leaving, the departing householders would place portraits of themselves or their relatives in the front windows of their apartments. The painted faces would gaze down the silent streets as a mute reproach to those who connived at the expulsions – their neighbours, some of whom must have approved of the new arrangements; others who simply did not care. As time passed, these images were bleached by the sun; the faces grew more and more washed out and haggard, and the rich hues of their clothes and surroundings faded. In less than a year, the portraits were almost unrecognizable, and in a majority of cases were no more than vague apparitions. But it was not before the vivid colour schemes had been rendered down to a monochrome, making some of the faces resemble death's heads, that people began to complain. It was as if every window had become a *memento mori*, solemnizing a House of the Dead. This was too much. What had seemed at first a vain and futile gesture was now an affront.

I remember, when I myself used to look out from The Astronomer's House on the central square of this city, I felt like a ghost appearing at the window. The windows in the other buildings were either unused or unusable. On the right-hand side was the main prison for the city and the region beyond it. On the left-hand side was the hospital, and opposite was the planetarium. The prison was a single large tower structure. The tower was round, with many barred windows, but these were now blind. In former times, the inmates had been in the habit of resting their arms on the sills and calling out to passers-by. Their speech had been coarse – even obscene –

and often aggressive or blasphemous. At a certain point the citizens organized a petition, and with the help of the clergy they forced the city fathers to put the convicts physically out of sight and hearing. A large metal duct was attached to each window, to muffle the sound from within. Each duct was open at the top – just enough to allow light and air to enter the cell. The only view now available to each prisoner was a narrow rectangle of sky, which never varied, except for the slow passage of clouds, or the rapid flight of birds.

The hospital was not purpose-built but the former palace of a disgraced noble. There were plenty of windows on the side facing the square, but all the rooms at the front were used by administrators, whose desks were placed sideways on to the view; while the windows on the sides of the building – and at the back – were set too high in the walls for the patients lying in bed to see anything but sections of brick wall in the building next door.

During my time in the hospital, I would spend much of the day looking at one square section of brick in this city while the sun would move all round the neighbouring building, roll over the slanting columns of fluted roof tiles – one after another – climb painstakingly over the curve of a gable and fall away from a projecting beam. At last, in the final minutes before twilight, it would throw a searchlight beam along the row of window sills where pigeons fight and push one another into the abyss. And then it would reach the back wall in this narrow courtyard and begin to siphon energy into this cold, unexposed core of the urban fabric. The light, distilled by the gauze of atmosphere and the urban canopy, the cloud cover and the drifting entrails of smoke, seemed purified now it had reached this destination. The brick would warm rapidly, purging shadows from its invisibly fractured surface, from all the vermicular defiles, ramps and gullies that first appeared with the brick's exit from the kiln. The heat would cling briefly to the walls of this microscopic maze and incubate everything inside it. Life stirred in the micro-cavities, though it could not remember instructions, could not remember the paths and directions it had taken during the last cycle of awakening. And then the light would start to dim.

The planetarium, of course, had no windows. It drew the cloak of night around those who stole inside, safe at last from the envy or disapproval of neighbours, colleagues and difficult relatives – the auditorium was large enough to accommodate everyone, even those who wished to escape to the furthest reaches of the galaxy. Once everyone had found their usual seat, the house lights would start to ebb and each dweller in the dark would yield to the steady onrush of the stars. Drifting in space, everyone was weightless, and every grudge, every impulse to resentment became pointless. All those unsatisfied longings simply floated away.

And time floated away, with its routines and pressures, as we watched the most distant stars, billions of years old, flicker and go out, while others surged into life. Sometimes the electricity supply was unreliable and the universe would suffer an eclipse, or glimmer uncertainly, but most often it would follow instructions and revolve obediently over our heads. But whatever the life span of the universe might be, the schedule of the planetarium was a certainty (barring the absence of staff, owing to illness or ebriety) and this was a great comfort, especially to the regulars. There were about a dozen of these at every performance, remaining in their seats when it ended and everyone else had departed. They would just sit there patiently in the twilight, hoping to be overlooked when the moment arrived for the staff to call them by name, before turning all the lights out, one by one.

But there is another square that I have to mention, a square comprising two fields close to the city centre; so close they are almost in the shadow of the great Tower of Culture. They cannot be seen from the surrounding streets, and even their nearest neighbours forget about them for years at a time. Visitors who climb the Tower to scan the metropolis for its architectural wonders overlook the fields, or construe them as remnants of an unsuccessful park, one that was swallowed up piecemeal by developers. But this is far from true – the fields have been farmed for a thousand years or more, and even now they are ploughed, sowed and harvested by a hard-shelled old man who has vowed never to sell up. By day, these fields go to sleep – they prefer to ignore the whirligig of human time, with its fuss and clamour and pointless sorties. But by night, they come alive, when the last creatures of their kind emerge into moonlight, and the insects glide among spires of grass, or finger their way over tapestries of roots, barricades of clay, or the endless underground galleries of their fossil relations.

There are no footpaths across, or alongside, the fields, but now and then, a local drunk is inspired to use them as a shortcut. He will stumble around for a bit, and end up in a ditch. But from there, lying on his back, he divines the true motions of the planets, and may even glimpse the fractions of another universe beyond ours. All the while, the earth is calculating his shape and weight and making ready to receive him, while the city is lost to thought, and the horizon all around is marked out by the black arms of field maples or the intricate tracery of a quickset hedge. And beyond them, there might as well be a forest, with wolves closing in, or a marshland with elk.

# Letter from Wales

## SAM ADAMS

The annual National Eisteddfod, as I have mentioned before, is a huge undertaking that taxes the energy and ingenuity of locations anxious to serve as host. This year it will be Pontypridd's turn, next Wrexham. In 1865, September 12–15, it was held at Aberystwyth. In early explorations of Aber during my first university term in 1952, I soon came across the stone circle erected for the opening ceremony of the 1865 'National' in the grounds of the ruined castle overlooking the seafront, adjacent to Hen Coleg, the oddly romantic old university building. So far as I can gather, the site chosen for that grand eisteddfodic occasion was a little distance from the castle – 'near the Market Hall', that week's *North Wales Chronicle* tells us. Judging from maps of the period this was probably at the junction of Market Street and Little Darkgate Street, rather than the town market's current location, then labelled 'Shambles' – clearly not at that period a salubrious spot. The *Chronicle* was impressed by the pavilion erected for the occasion, 'a magnificent structure... 36 yards wide by 50 long' affording a platform thirty feet by fifty feet. Elsewhere we are told it was nothing but 'a skeleton of poles, beams, and rafters covered with an impervious coating of felt' with 'sheets of delicate canvas' at intervals to let a little daylight enter. The interior was decorated with national flags, 'festoons of laurels... (and) the shields of the fifteen tribes of Wales'. It had seating for four thousand and, undeterred by the long hours of travel involved, crowds 'to marvel at' came daily from all over mid- and north Wales to pack the auditorium, despite weather during this period 'so hot as to be almost unbearable'. How many were attracted by publicity boasting that Prince Louis Lucien Napoleon, a spare-time researcher in European Celtic connections, would attend as an adjudicator of entries for a literary competition we cannot know. In the event, he pleaded indisposition and sent his apologies. But despite difficulties endured in deciphering some of the handwriting, he had read the entries for the set topic, 'Origin of the English Nation', and delivered his critique by post, which was that all were 'more or less weak'. His absence was a grave disappointment, 'like Hamlet without the Prince', the president for the session commented. David Davies ('Llandinam' is invariably added to distinguish him from others bearing the same name), the hugely successful coal and rail entrepreneur, presiding at another session and, speaking in Welsh, told the audience, to cheers and applause, that 'the best medium to make money by was English; and he would advise every one of his countrymen to master it perfectly'. It was a milestone in the long retreat of the Welsh language.

At the same 'National', the verdict of judges on the few entries for the major poetry competition, 'the Chair', an awdl composed in the ancient, strict bardic metres on the subject Hanes Paul (the history of St Paul) was 'neb yn deilwng' (no-one worthy) and the prize was withheld, always a grave disappointment. Among competitors for the lesser lyrical poetry prize (three guineas!) on the subject Y Fodrwy Briodasol, (The Wedding Ring) were Islwyn (Thomas Williams, 1832–78) and Ceiriog (John Ceiriog Hughes, 1832–87), both already marked for literary fame, but they were beaten on this occasion by a poet with the ffug-enw (false name) 'Muta' – which, rather than Welsh, seems to have been an ironic classical reference to a female figure rendered mute. Thus Sarah Jane Rees (1839–1916) found her voice, became the first woman to win a prize for poetry at the Eisteddfod with a poem expressing her dissatisfaction with the conventional role of women, and revealed to the wider world one facet of an extraordinary array of talents. On the net you will find her collected poems entitled *Caniadau* ('Songs': undated, but 1870). Though hardly 'songs' of the conventional, brief lyrical sort, the collection showcases elements of the bardic role of memoriser and celebrator of local people, places and events, and boldly displays the ffug-enw 'Cranogwen', derived in the more conventional bardic way from her birthplace, Llangrannog, some thirty miles south of Aberystwyth down the coast of Cardigan Bay, now justly famed among the youth of Wales as the home of the Urdd summer camps. The baptismal name has been largely forgotten: it is as Cranogwen that she is now known and celebrated. The Aber 'National' was not the end of her competitive career as poet – she won a prize of two guineas for another lyric, on Hiraeth ('Longing for home'), again no doubt written meaningfully, when the Eisteddfod went over the border to Chester in 1866, and the Chair at an Eisteddfod in Aberaeron in 1872 – but that was not all. She had different ambitions, and immense personal conviction and drive to achieve them.

She was born in 1837, the daughter of Frances and John Rees, who describes himself in the 1851 Census as a 'Master Mariner' and captained a ketch plying up and down the coast and occasionally across to Ireland. Her date of birth is confirmed in the 1841 Census, when her father was absent, presumably on sea, and she had two older brothers. Later Census returns make her two or even three years younger. Her father's cargoes were usually salt for preserving fish, chalk to burn to lime for the fields, and coal dust to mix with clay as cheap fuel. He was not wealthy: the family lived in one half of a thatched cottage a couple of miles up the valley from the sea. He was reputedly a drinker, but took pains to teach his daughter before she attended classes given by a retired schoolmaster. Her formal education began in local elementary schools, but with experience of shipboard life and work, at first with her father, she progressed to nautical school in London and Liverpool and, in turn, she too qualified as a master mariner.

But with that achievement she seems to have declared herself satisfied and seafaring no longer a challenge. There were other goals. She was a schoolteacher and then head of a school for a dozen years. In 1879 she became the first woman in Wales to edit a women's magazine, *Y Frythones* ('British Woman') which, we are told, among other things campaigned for girls' education, and she became a highly popular public speaker. As a lecturer at home and twice among the Welsh-speakers of the United States, she carried the message of Temperance. Back on her home patch, the local *Welsh Gazette* in August 1905 noted that Cranogwen had visited several times and a branch of the

South Wales Temperance Union, which she had founded, had been started at Henllan to which 'all lady reformers [were] cordially invited'. There were a hundred and forty branches in South Wales by the time she died.

Through all the travel, the changing circumstances, Llangranog remained 'home', as the decennial census reveals. In 1891, when she was fifty-two, she is declared head of the household rather than her widower father, then eighty-four. She still resided at 'Green Park, Llangrannog Henllan' in 1911, but her preaching tours continued: she died on the road, at Cilfynydd, a mining village in South Wales, and was brought home to be buried in St Crannog's churchyard. A statue of her was recently unveiled at the Community Garden, Llangrannog.

## Ochre Pitch

### HAL COASE

Earlier versions of six of these stanzas originally appeared in *Prototype 5* (Prototype: London, 2023)

There is a selflessness in any past, at root,
it will not fold. Tonight, there are the pines
placed as though falling for each other
and across the way, the neighbouring roof
snubs a sky of blues and an excitable red.
I would like to give this light a name, call it
something, learn it good. But it won't answer.
It only gives itself, beside the water pump,
which rattles on: *enough, enough, enough*

I had taken the ferry, and on the ferry, Chiara
had said: the colony. And I had said: family album,
roots, schooling, tea and jam, the white veranda
on which my uncle and his brother are burning
citronella oil to keep mosquitoes at bay, while nana
cricks a cigarette in a gloved hand, years learning
to hide inside that smoke. At 5am sharp: Tavolara,
the ochre of its cliffs pitched up towards a sky
marbled pink and pressing into wideness.

that this new tongue I have is bedded on your
kindnesses. I mean the kindness of a lemon tree
you planted three years ago in a garden without
much grammar or adequate soil but astonishingly
braved by life: green and gem yellows cowled
at this hour by the mountain that we're climbing
tomorrow. It is a tongue that can be powerless,
broken and shared out like a stack of *carasau*,
a kind of passing tribute to the land's curve south.

the day we arrive, forty years since they bombed
Bologna centrale. Don't spare me the violence
of this talk, or think that we can do it honestly
with words. We will talk it out, driving less
at the event, more at its incredibility, the long
pain of knowing why, when, how, and guessing
who's to blame. A show of guilt which wrongs
the innocent, who have no use for explanations
and would have lived without commemoration.

We walk down to Cala Luna. The scale of it all
is overturned: each stone an island, the island
one stone. Pines that syllable the old trail
with their needling, a trail that pipes in a wind
as bold and slight as the lizard's going sparkle.
Disordered words that land on sea prickled
ears, until it all sounds one rocking laughter.
You, setting out the coffee flask in a cave
above, and I catch only: *Kafka is in love.*

We're going inland to hunt for some *Nuraghe*,
in your dad's car, with a map that plots the castles
as blue huts next to picnic spots and panorama.
Your town slides off, one garage and flag at a time.
I pick out the way that the builder-giants roamed
when there were builders, we could say, if taken by
some myth-trodden dream of hurt and gloominess.
The brace of old faces in the bars that stare down
the sun clawing its way into their awninged lair.

Way out, past the careful plots and subplots
and fenced peripheries, there is a wedding scene,
a village come out to cheer on what may be love,
comedy of efforts and care. A knowing tendency,
that queer habit of doubt, pinches our wonder
just as we notice that smoke is wheeling up
there, where a forest is cut back to jolts of wood
in this valley cleared for centuries, still home
to a joy and a music that not one of us owns.

A landscape bitten to the edge of abstraction,
not loved, but prised of love, and not named,
not even traced in letters but like the seathreads
that lap and clothe this island dressing whoever
should need it. The radio brings disaster's progress.
The sky, adjusted for contaminants, shivers out
the awns and then distends its sickbay drape
around the old orange cork trees, severed
down the middle with such caesarean exactness

that the mere immediacy of sight is punctured.
There is an anger in everything. The corks
ripped from their bristled jackets, bellies nude
and pocked with climbing dew, lean to earth –
miserable heroes on blunt swords of shade.
A neutrality collapses. You narrate the war
that put NATO on the coast. On your word,
two fighter jets rise – bulls of foam in unbearable
suspension – barrel over us, cordage strained

to break. The sky reels in its loafing clouds,
spread like cattle cut to bloodless chunks
by a madman's axe. Then a thin quiet ploughs
the roadside, ruts the very air with a sunless
calm, as the blue of Gioacchino's dream rounds
the mountain. We two peasants pause to piss
on a dry stone wall, splashing the thirsty grass,
the car crouched back, picking up its blissed
out tunes again. Then, you: look, there it is.
                                        *eccolo*

There, ahead of us, down the valley, we do not
find a fortress. What I had thought would be
a towering thing was a handsome bag of stone,
a botched minaret, a sandcastle knocked down
on a prehistoric shore. We hop the gate
and stalk towards it as if the walls could rouse.
There is a ginnel of dark to enter in, a nostril
taking air and making sense of it. You first,
you first – your smile smarts then vanishes.

What we know in the dark is how to last,
the patience of stone and tang of bird shit
underfoot, the loss of your face sharpened
on memory, summer skin lapsing into dust.
How to last out together, even when apart,
even when, trespassers in the monster's hut,
we are of manner more than two: father,
friend, disasters, whatever is left of the light
that gets in and seams the soil so tight.

Light brittle with evening, the late sun
excludes its ends, lying rich in a hoofmark
or the bags of your eyes. The palms listen
on the stone, touch probes for guesswork,
slate and salt, whatever it is weakening
into tender muck. Estuaries of song:

        there is a brick floating on the river,
        there is the river holding a brick,
        there is us comprehending the risk.

Why heroic? *I couldn't give a fuck.*
Your answer is always a diver's launch
        into blue, a brushstroke's urgent
parallel to blue, a sea-caught
        bob of hair, long arms bent,
that little sweep a hemistich, not
        stopping but allowing pause,
or the break, always to break,
        the gratitude that floats on blue.

The grammar that arranges our departures
tells us nothing of arrival. The drive back
we make the circumference of the drive out,
as though the centre had dispersed, black
and free into the fields of juniper sprouts,
out to a tidewrack with its plastics and weeds.

Keep on the horizon, everything pronounces,
and as you pass me on that scrap of Gramsci,
evening comes up with a bone in its mouth.

the part artifice of morning breath and
rain packed in overnight giddy up sunrise
a movement down in the kitchen a lesson
on maps (that they age quite suddenly)
a loan bit of hair a brush of fox marks
the day set like a copper bust of night
a woman laughs pragmatically outside
not knowing the future's real charm
the kettle whining out its false alarm

A space unconditional: a better idea
        than the few beats of tolerance
we tend to give ourselves. How to hear
        the moth last night? Errant as
a loanword, I half woke on its weakness,
        its awful breathy sand along
the walls. It was before me, then left
        us separate, and we slept.

I, too, dislike most finished things, even if
the lake we circled today had a finish to it,
mirroring its banks up to a truss bridge
that trapped a scarce cloud. It's our chat
of small cares and goings on that sounds
like March, with its new fever, insistent
that the middles of camellias brave it out,
their redness coming on with the first fly
at home to take the temperature of fruit.

# Of Queerness

## GREGORY WOODS

Early in the 1980s, Nikos Stangos said to Robert K. Martin, author of *The Homosexual Tradition in American Poetry* (1979), 'Literature is literature... There is no such thing as gay literature'. Stangos, a poet who was gay, was the commissioning editor with responsibility for the Penguin Modern Poetry (Ashbery, Ginsberg, Harwood...) and Penguin Modern European Poetry (Cavafy, Pessoa, Ritsos, Tsvetaeva...) series. Gay/lesbian poets are only great if you don't categorise them as such. Djuna Barnes said, 'I am not a lesbian, I just loved Thelma', either meaning that she only ever loved one woman in that way, or that she declined to be treated as a case study in a category of supposed deviancy. In 1987, Yves Navarre responded to an invitation to a conference of lesbian/gay writers: 'I am gay, I am a writer, I am not a gay writer.' Indeed, one can hardly blame those who reject the category 'lesbian/gay writer' when they are working within a homophobic value system.

So who is what? Adrienne Rich famously developed the idea of the 'lesbian continuum', involving 'a range – through each woman's life and throughout history – of woman-identified experience, not simply the fact that a woman has had or consciously desired genital sexual experience with another woman' ('Compulsory Heterosexuality and Lesbian Existence', 1980). As Olga Broumas pointed out, referring to Rich's 'Twenty-One Love Poems', 'It is not the physical which defines this love as lesbian, but the absolute and primary attention directed at the other' – and the other is a woman. We are reminded of Audre Lorde's espousal of the old Carriacou name for women who work and live together as friends and lovers, Zami.

The continuum allows Emily Dickinson a substantial role in any serious discussion of lesbian poetry. We might even make room for Edith Sitwell ('I write in the rhythms of Sappho, though I do not have that lady's unfortunate disposition') for her own gender-queer performativity and prolific alliances across the spectra. Yet there are still those who demand, as it were, the definitive proof of physical activity, the 'smoking dildo' (to use Hilary McCollum's fragrant expression). When Auden says 'The proofs of love have had to be destroyed' ('Dear to me now...'), I think of the ashes of Byron's memoirs, cooling in John Murray's grate. Even where there was telling evidence, it generally had to be erased. In the face of centuries of such imposed silences, gay readers cannot be expected to go rummaging through every writer's linen like the chambermaid who reported, of Oscar Wilde's hotel bed, that 'The sheets were stained in a peculiar way'. Walt Whitman's claim of having fathered six children tells us nothing to disavow, still less to disprove, the homoeroticism of the 'Calamus' or 'Drum-Taps' poems. Yet the lack of those proofs is often held against us. In my view, the onus should be on the deniers to come up with evidence – and what disproof could there possibly be?

Rich was thinking of the particular circumstances of women's lives, but her broader argument makes no less sense when applied to men. As the anonymous author of 'Don Leon' (fancied by some to be Lord Byron) wrote: 'Oh! 'tis hard to trace / The line where love usurps tame friendship's place'. Umberto Saba thought flexibly in terms of 'amicizia amorosa'. Roland Barthes argued that we should speak of 'homosexualities', plural. The expansion of the designation LGBTQ+, over the past three decades, has happened in a similar spirit. Queer intersects with other otherings, including that of (oh, horror!) sexlessness.

Deducing that Fernando Pessoa probably never had sex with another person, his biographer Richard Zenith seems to conclude that he cannot be described as hetero- or homosexual, nor even as bisexual. 'There is no secret Pessoa for the biographer to reveal.' Since this argument rules out the possibility of an inner life – still less of Pessoa's multiple inner lives – I asked Zenith about this, in person at a bookshop event, and found that this is, indeed, his understanding of the case. This decision leaves him ill-equipped to imagine Pessoa's fear of exposure; let alone 'the insatiable, unquantifiable longing to be both the same and other' (*The Book of Disquiet*); let alone the strategies of distancing and dissembling that might arise from both the tragedy of a homosexual man cornered into celibacy and the comedy of a man performing alternative identities to confound his enemies and amuse himself. (Saying that Gerard Manley Hopkins had no sexual orientation because he had no sex life would be, apart from any other consideration, to erase the sheer destructive effort, and creative effect, of his celibacy, which would thereby be diluted to an inconvenience.) The lack of firm evidence of physical activity has similarly allowed various critics to deduce from the solitude of Emilio Prados, in part caused by illness, that he was not homosexual. I have never seen this logic applied to a heterosexual individual. Besides, even unloved, one can love: Pedro Homem de Mello addresses a billet-doux to his own loneliness ('Solidão').

Since parents tend not to bring us up as ourselves, and academic syllabuses are still generally silent on our lives, lesbians and gay men have had to be autodidacts to get to know our own culture. Audre Lorde: 'We are learning by heart / what has never been taught' ('Call'). Muriel Rukeyser speaks of a 'bed of forbidden things finally known' ('The Transgress'). What was once unspeakable comes to be spoken: for, in some sense, 'Nothing is until it has been said' (Maureen Duffy, 'I Love You'). To explore our own culture, we have to be able to find it in the first place, so we excavate our lost histories and trace our ancestral descent. My own last collection was a haiku-less tribute to Matsuo Bashō. As well as reasserting, and connecting with, our presence in cultural history, this is also a question of writing ourselves into the mainstream.

In the late 1970s I wrote a doctoral thesis on homoerotic poetry. After a survey of common themes, it had individual chapters on Lawrence, Crane, Auden, Ginsberg and Gunn. It was revised and published as *Articulate Flesh: Male Homo-eroticism and Modern Poetry, 1914–1980* (Yale, 1987). There, as in my later work, by concentrating on the needs and experiences of the 'gay reader', I allowed myself, for better or worse, to sidestep the strict inhibitions of social constructionist queer theory with regard to the existence of 'homosexuality' in periods prior to the development of that concept in the late 1800s. I glibly wrote: 'A gay text is one which lends itself to the hypothesis of a gay reading, regardless of where the author's genitals were wont to keep house.' Gay and lesbian readers, in my view, were to be encouraged to recognise themselves – their own patterns of emotion and desire – in their readings of Sappho, Theocritus, Richard Barnfield, Katherine Philips, Bashō – while still distinguishing our times and places from theirs. (I have never seen much reason to stray from this view. Although I taught queer theory for decades, in my own work I always gave it a light touch.) Nor was proof of sexual activity a requirement to merit a writer's inclusion among those who could be read as gay. This recognition of gay readers' agency has always irritated some non-gay readers (if that is what they are). Jeffrey Meyers said of my book: 'Woods's special pleading and specious arguments – primarily intended, as his style suggests, for a homosexual audience – are unlikely to convince an objective reader.' I like to imagine that being said about French readers of French literature.

Of course, Meyers's claim to objectivity is close kin to the colonising of the 'universal' for restricted interests. When I (male) write a love poem about 'him', is my poem less good than if I said 'you'? Would this also be the case if I said 'she' instead? (Or, for that matter, 'they' singular.) In this context, the assessors of quality tend to be asking which mode is the more 'universal'. This is not a question of statistics: that heterosexuality may be more common than homosexuality does not make it the slightest bit more universal. In 1988, Édouard Roditi wrote to correct me about the use of the ungendered 'you' in his love poems. Harold Norse had drawn his attention to my claim, in *Articulate Flesh*, that he (Roditi) expected his readers to infer a 'he' from his uses of 'you'. I had quoted a claim of his, in a 1978 article in *Gay Sunshine*, that a gay poet's omission of a specified gender from his love poems 'should distinguish it clearly from the love poems of most heterosexual poets, who rarely leave the reader in doubt about the sex of their Celia, Clelia, Delia, Dark Rosaleen or Lalage'. He was referring specifically to poems 'on homosexual themes' that he, Auden and Spender wrote in the 1930s. I had mischievously commented: 'If this is the understanding on which such poems were written – if the reader was meant to infer that "you" meant "he" – the universalising factor ceases to function'. Deliberately not stating crucial social details in order to achieve universality seemed to me, itself, to convey a crucial social detail (enforced discretion) that is no more universal than openness would have been in the first place. Roditi and I crossed purposes a couple of times each before getting on with our lives.

Today, we have additional pronoun debates – on the use of the unsexed, non-binary, singular 'they', for instance. One might ask what is lost to the specifics of erotic writing by the use of nondescript pronouns. Yet it can be done: 'Of hand, of foot, of lip, of eye, of brow' (Shakespeare, sonnet 106). Besides, English has survived a previous loss of distinctions (thou/you) and may even have gained by the consequent ambiguities of distance. The new usage of 'they' could have the effect of calling the bluff of older traditions of 'androgyny' and 'sexual ambiguity', which were rarely any such thing.

The supposedly double-sexed nature of the gay or lesbian body was always metaphorical; but what if the bothness, or its ghostly twin neitherness, were to become literal – 'as if we dreamed ourselves into being / and this was forbidden' (Clare Shaw, 'On Being Trans')? The publication of Janice Raymond's book *The Transsexual Empire* (1979), pointedly subtitled *The Making of the She-Male*, set off an impassioned debate between pro-and anti-trans factions within our communities. But because these discussions took place in person, or at least, when in print, under real names, there were tears and anger but, as far as I can recall, no death threats. This was just as well, really, since it was our progressive alliances, even across fundamental disagreements, that would, within a handful of years, protect us against the plague of homophobia accompanying the AIDS epidemic. The debate between radical feminism and the trans movement, which was negotiated politely for decades, has now been taken over by outside interests and weaponised accordingly. The more that trans lives are caught up in the hyperbolic intransigence of social media, the more they deserve the cleaner lines of (let's call it) poetic engagement. Joelle Taylor: 'If we were to regain the real-life meeting-grounds, if we were to be in the same room, then perhaps we would remember our commonality. The internet celebrates difference. The [LGBTQ] club celebrates unity. In these distinct spaces we learn to protect one another. We learn that we are one another.'

This sense of protective, shared subcultures has long been contested, though. Visiting New York in 1929, Lorca was thrilled by the Whitmanliness of the men in the streets, but deplored the evidence he saw of a separate subculture of 'fairies' ('madres de fango', he called them in an enraged, homophobic slur, distancing himself from sodomy: mothers of mud, meaning shit). Other visitors too (Mishima, Pasolini) distinguished between good homoeroticism, opportunities among beautiful men in the streets and parks, and the bad gay ghetto. This is partly a contrast between indoor and outdoor cruising, but also between straight masculinity (available to the eye and more) and gay effeminacy. In his 1944 essay 'The Homosexual in Society', Robert Duncan deplores 'the cultivation of a secret language, the *camp*, a tone and a vocabulary that is loaded with contempt

for the human', even going so far as to add that 'this cult' plays 'an evil role in society'.

Loosely applying his reservations to poetry, Duncan distinguishes between unnamed separatists and the single case of Hart Crane: 'Where the Zionists of homosexuality have laid claim to a Palestine of their own, asserting in their miseries their nationality, Crane's suffering, his rebellion, and his love are sources of poetry for him not because they are what makes him different from, superior to, mankind, but because he saw in them his link with mankind; he saw in them his sharing in universal human experience.' Contrary even to his own career, Duncan suggests that the universal can only be achieved by becoming indistinguishable.

But Camp is neither secret nor monolithic. Its styles, tones and idioms are many: think of Oscar Wilde, Stefan George, Gertrude Stein, Cocteau, Lorca, Auden, Edith Sitwell, Frank O'Hara, James Merrill, John Ashbery, Assotto Saint, Jeremy Reed, Mark Doty, John McCullough… Robert Duncan himself. In Wilde's day, Camp developed around *paradoxical* responses to conventionality. In the last chapter of my book *A History of Gay Literature: The Male Tradition* (Yale, 1998), I identified the creative incompatibilities of paradox as the trope most aptly representative of homosexuality as distinct from the tautologies of heterosexuality (e.g. male + female = reproduction). In a cross-cultural and trans-historical sequence of generalisations – this was my book's closing peroration – I cited Shakespeare's Achilles and Patroclus (hiding in their tent 'to make paradoxes') and Balzac's Vautrin ('il entend bien le paradoxe'); as well as Byron, Whitman and Pasolini's assertions of the necessary right to contradict themselves (Pasolini: 'Lo scandalo del contraddirmi'). One man's simple statement of lived experience is another's outrage against natural logic: 'For my Other is not a woman but a man' (Robert Duncan, 'The Torso').

Although Thom Gunn was one of the writers who first led me to this conclusion, when I showed him an earlier version of the argument, in 1989, Gunn disagreed with me on it, especially for my rather flaky claim that scientific discourse eschews the paradoxical. Gunn had developed a poetry of normative masculinity (soldiers, bikers, Elvis…) to suit the style of his own gayness while implicitly repudiating not only supposed sissies like Stephen Spender but gay culture's uses of Camp. Yet Gunn was once happy to apply the epithet 'High Camp' to Ben Jonson's 'Elegie on the Lady Jane Pawlet', adding: 'What we must remember is that artifice is not necessarily the antithesis of sincerity' (*The Occasions of Poetry*). Camp's love of artifice takes *contra naturam* to one of its logical conclusions. And the idea that we ourselves are contradictions in terms has not vanished as laws, customs and attitudes have liberalised to our benefit. You need only consider the intractably perplexing conundrum the Church of England sees in same-sex marriage, or the Twittersphere in the lives of trans people, where the rest of us see, and experience, them as unexceptional facts of our quotidian routines. We are 'birds of paradox' (Joelle Taylor, 'Got a Light, Jack?').

Homophobia is one of the crucial themes in LGBTQ writing; it hardly needs saying. Cavafy responds to press reports of a murder ('The News Item'). Antonio Botto identifies with an individual who caves in to homophobic pressure: 'I've left my beloved forever, / I've already bowed to the world's demand' ('Já deixei o meu amor, / já fiz a vontade ao mundo'). Mark Doty responds to hostile graffiti ('Homo Shall Not Inherit'). David Tait laments the Pulse nightclub massacre in Florida ('After Orlando'). The poetry of the AIDS epidemic was as much about homophobia as it was about love and loss. Indeed, it was reviewed accordingly: Thom Gunn wrote to me, apropos of *The Man with Night Sweats*, 'I have found that the reviewers like reading about *dead* queers. Quite acceptable, that' (17 June 1992). Our rehabilitation of the old insult 'queer' happened at the worst stage of the epidemic. It was meant to sound angrier and, indeed, more perverse than either the official, medico-legal term 'homosexual' or even than 'lesbian/gay'. It was used to describe radical political strategies and the vulnerability of psyches and physiques in extremis. It was, perforce, explicit about bodily parts, functions and activities, pleasures and pains; explicit, also, about emotions that gay liberation had tried to downplay: terror, loneliness, regret, shame.

In expressions and representations of shame – the body assailed by AIDS and stigmatised by hostility to AIDS, the abjection of the transitional body, the great set pieces of performative humiliation in Genet – we always find the tell-tale boot print of homophobia. Shame remains active, therefore, in the narratives of our lives. We find it in the three dimensions of time: our past (Danez Smith: 'many stories about queerness are about shame'), present (Richard Scott: 'free from shame but made from shame') and future (Gregory Woods: 'let me keep my shame'). The word comes at us in flurries when Andrew McMillan addresses adolescence. In a liberated context, the individual might feel shame for past compliance: 'Trust me I know what it is to be alive, but I smothered it in normal' (Kae Tempest).

Stephen Spender once wrote to me, apropos of the Italian youths in my first collection, *We Have the Melon*: 'You are warm about them [,] you embrace them but you do not want to redeem them. You don't have a christian attitude about them', adding: 'In similar circumstances I would probably have a christian attitude' (11 August 1989). Indeed, nothing could be further from my own attitude. If anyone needed redeeming it was me; and if anyone could do it, they could. They released me from my own shame, the product of external and internalised homophobia. In the end, shame can be rendered triumphant, as in Rimbaud's gang-rape poem 'Le cœur supplicié'. Shamed but not ashamed. 'Ultimate shame, consummate bliss!' (Mikhail Kuzmin). 'Shame, too, makes identity' (Eve Kosofsky Sedgwick).

Manuel Forcano: 'What will we not do for love' ('Què no fem per amor'). With histories like ours, we are sure of two things: love is difficult, but it is always worth fighting for. Given the continuing global context of homophobic and transphobic violence, abuse and censorship, queer writing has a strong record of hopes for progressive, future social change. Walt Whitman: 'I will make divine magnetic lands, / With the love of comrades, / With the life-long love of comrades' ('For You, O Democracy'). When Vicente Aleixandre declares that the time for kissing is not ripe ('el tiempo de los besos no ha llegado') and then Lorca quotes him for one of the epigraphs in *Poeta en Nueva York*, both imply a future ripe with kisses. Even Cavafy manages an optimistic impulse: 'Later, in a more perfect society, / surely some other person created like me / will appear and act freely' ('Hidden Things', trans. Rae Dalven). There is always much to be defended, more to be achieved. 'The queer poem, then, is hopeful. As I write, the queer poem is a wish which stems from a desire' (Mary Jean Chan, 'Ars Poetica'). Or, indeed, from desire in general. It still celebrates 'All things counter, original, spare, strange' (Hopkins, 'Pied Beauty'), including 'New thresholds, new anatomies!' (Hart Crane, 'The Wine Menagerie').

In 1928, under the eyes of the secret police, Mikhail Kuzmin gave what turned out to be his last poetry recital to a packed hall in Leningrad, reading from his collection *The Trout Breaks the Ice*, with its themes of same-sex love. Something went wrong with the allocation of tickets and what the student organisers had tried to prevent did happen: the hall, already packed, was invaded by a crowd of homosexual men ('undesirables') bearing flowers, with which they pelted the poet when he finished reading. One of the organisers called it 'the last demonstration of Leningrad's homosexuals'. I like to think of this mixed audience of ticket-holders and gate-crashers, scholars and aesthetes, intellectuals and activists, all contributing to the same ovation, all on the same side against repressive forces, as representing the routinely compatible differences of progressive readership.

# Five Poems

## ALEX MICHAEL STANLEY

### Night Air

300 miles west, the sun is caught
mid-dive into a faraway ocean.
The ancient 'either, or' of duty and love
has come to bite me in the ass.
I've lost both, I'm sorry, mortal ears fall short.
I thought life to be more a puzzle than a maze,
I thought the relapse a coincidence,
I thought she could lead me to you.

Only the desert will claim me now,
my old master who sees more for me
than singing for rain as the light disappears,
the light in the dark cradling stars,
behind the same mountains,
while patience graciously sifts through
the night air, telling me to hold fast
and watch each mountain tremble.

### Western Slope

*Silverton, Colorado*

An old hunter drives past me in a beat-up pickup truck,
kicking dust as he bumps his way to a hunting ground.
At night, I hear gunshots on the other side of the valley,
long after dusk. At dawn, something wanders
past my tent. What did I think this would be?
My mission to pen a love letter to my country
became a city boy lost in a wild world.
I thought I'd write ballads about the tall grass,
not the fear that a lack of cell phone reception brings.
Yet, I have no home except for this forest of rooms,
the mossen floor enchanting and vibrant.
I make my way through it, through the rain,
in the middle of it, in the middle of the forest,
past where the dirt road is broken by a new creek,
past where the other side ends, past the clearings,
a half-mile past the river, I find a collapsed shack.
It is broken to pieces, flattened by the elements,
old and forgotten. I bid to imagine how it got here
in the first place. Even my imagination falls short.
I see a broken furnace and wonder where the kitchen is,
the living room. I listen for echoes of the life once here.
I strain, until I hear the river say that nothing has changed.

## Ruin, *Wijiji*

There is no more water in this canyon,
no spouts after a gentle tap on the rock.
The nothing of space I stand within hollowed
as millennia slid into the present. We share
a moment of weakness, daring against the sun,
praying a little water might sustain forever,
since the mountains and stone glow
with the color of home. Yellow sand sifts through
the shavings of arrowheads, each tip pointing
in its intended direction. I stand above
oceanic proportions of rock, in a place
the heron would visit each autumn in droves,
now only hawks and crows to watch the banks,
sunken into shrubbery, into a sneer, like a bone
too far into the earth for anyone to know.
Cracked pottery sits atop the ground, distinct
with painted dots and lines, its curve, that of a plate,
these days holding futility in a layer of dust.
I've given an old life to be here, to avoid a death
of misplaced pride, so as not to miss what the others do,
to listen for the water before looking for the mountains
and the canyon walls. I hear the thunderbird's
dry croak. I stand in ruin and call it home.

## Spirit Line

*Death Valley, California*

Death is pale on the other side of darkness,
like the ghosts made of salt that wander
across these roads. This whole valley
is a mirage, the salt deposits hold
the visage of a sea once here,
now gone. In the afternoon sun,
the dunes make perfect triangles,
the thin brush near the road is dusted white,
and the mountains beyond are scraped
of their green. At night, mules bray
like seals, now fossils, and the gods
switch faces behind the stars.

## Breaking into Tor House

*Carmel-by-the-Sea, California*

A stone cottage and a stone tower,
sit side-by-side on the Pacific coast,
built by the poet Robinson Jeffers
for his wife, Una, each piece of granite
hauled from the slope of beach below.

At 3am, I can only see the two buildings
as tombstones, the wedded pair is buried
in the courtyard with unmarked graves
beneath a yew tree, the same tree
Celtic legend says will bring one back to life.

I step out of my lightless truck, hop
over the gap in the front gate, haggle
with the gate at the succeeding fence,
before jumping over that, too. It's easy
enough to navigate under the full moon.

The tower windows look fed by oil,
the sky's tide crashing into the light.
People say they've seen ghosts here,
specifically, Una, the more outspoken
of the two, walking the tower steps, posing

in the background of photos, knocking
books from their shelves, defending
Robinson's legacy – muse, manager, partner.
They settled here when it was just themselves,
this barren cliff, the Pacific, granite, fog.
I might know more, though yesterday

I was barred from entering after missing
the last tour of the day, driving eight hours
across the state, to be left at the front gate,
peering in while the tour guide's lips move.

I know when poets are told they cannot,
they do only that, building castles by the sea,
crafting silent monuments, planting trees
where only weeds grow, or, they come back
to hop a fence once the neighborhood has lulled.

The courtyard brick here is pristine, gardens in order,
stone resting. The moon could simply cast a reflection
into a figured, flowing, blurrily gowned woman.
I want to see something, anything to reverse my belief,
to give a story before the fire turns into coals.

I stand before Hawk Tower. It is said Una performed
séances in a second story room. I call to her from below,
'Una, descend the stairs, I am only a young poet
seeking.' The sea answers. There is no other sound,
no spirit yawning, no owl rustling to look from its hole.

A few steps forward, into the alcove to the tower door.
I enter its shadow, press on the wood. Granite cracks –
a voice deep from the sea said, 'You don't need my help.'

# On Risk!

## Carl Phillips and the Poetry of Feeling

### KIRSTY GUNN

Earlier this year I woke in the middle of the night unable to breathe. I lay in the dark, alert, aware of every single intake of air and its expulsion. I was alone. I was in a remote place. There was no one to take me to hospital or order a car or ambulance, and nothing I could do except lie very still and quiet until the episode passed and I could feel my body returning to its nomal resting state.

It occurs to me now, as I start to write this piece about the poetry of Carl Phillips, that those feelings I had in that faraway house, in that deep midnight of a room, reflect exactly the state I am in when reading the work of this powerfully affective writer. There's something heavy resting on my chest; my heart rate increases. 'The wind stirred – the water beneath it stirred accordingly' Phillips writes in 'Speak Low'. For long seconds I am conscious of my body and the poem that is before me in the most scary, acute, unsettled kind of way.

None of this is to say his work carries dread, of some dire warning, portent of illness or incapacity, or of an existential kind. On the contrary, these are poems filled with life, with love and sense and physicality and knowledge of pleasure. Oh, yes. Pleasure. Masses of good, bodily, emotionally charged physical pleasure. So – gardens. Trees. Men. Fruit. Animals. The light itself. The temperature... All are felt as sensation, experience, lust in the way Robert Herrick framed his lust for life in his poems, all the many minutes of it. So, 'Having opened to their fullest, they opened further –' we read in 'Distortion'. 'Now the peonies, near to breaking, splay groundward [...] they're not the not-so-lovely-after-all example / of how excess, even in its smallest forms, seems to have / its cost [...] his smell / on you after, like those parts of the gutted deer that / the men bring home with them'. And, later, 'it's a distortion of the will / that leads to passion' – as though the seventeenth-century poet's same compression of time into moments of awareness and fullness gives us 'The light at this late-afternoon hour when it works both / against and in the body's favor'.

So yes, they make me feel thrilled to be alive, these sonnets and lyrics and odes; I am in the company of one who knows how to test feeling and feeling's limits, to extract from targeted sensation and from involvement in the world in general the most precise and yet wildly generative, richly allusive imaginative response. In 'All the Love You've Got' there's this:

> And now, having dismissed everyone as he
> wishes he could dismiss his own dreams
>     that make each
> night restless – that same unswayable
>     knowledge, and
> the belief in it, that he is

> king here, which means
> being a stranger, at least outwardly, to even the least
> trace of doubt – after all of this, the king has
>     stepped
> from the royal tent, is walking toward the sound
>     of water...

And in 'Honest in Which Not Gently', there is 'Panicking too late, as is / the way with panic... that feels like ritual and a release from ritual' which makes me think also – in company with Herrick but so different from him – of George Herbert and his 'The Pulley', a poem about which Phillips has written, attending altogether in his verse and prose to the poetic work of that late Renaissance period and finding, in its charged ambivalences between bodily capture and soul's flight, congruence and affiliation.[1] The same pull and release function is at work in Phillips's 'They say language has its own sorrow / but no word for it; does this crying out maybe come close, though, / can we say it does, to have stared into the dark and said aloud, even / if quietly, Who's there?'. The same machine that drives the verse also drives its powerful subject – 'like being lost,' Phillips writes, 'but free.'

The dread I feel, then, the overwhelming sense of being enthralled by these poems, reminds me of an attack of breathlessness in the middle of the night, of being held fast, in a closed-off, timeless zone before being let go, flung back into the breathing air that is like the white space at the bottom of the page. Though it seems so startling and pressing and contemporary, the feeling might not be new to me after all. Because of Herbert. Herrick. John Donne. Henry Vaughan. How they do take their place here, bodies and souls, their sensibilities and emblems of belief and desire enmeshed within the workings of Phillips's own exquisite poetics. There is a similar arrangement of emotion that I experience in the long seconds of my attention being fastened in place as a kind of energy kept in reserve, banked up, resisted. The air drawn out of me... but then, with the acceptance of such restriction, pleasure; release.

---

1 'On Risk' is the title of an essay that was the first thing by Carl Phillips that I ever read – before I met his poetry. It is in a collection called 'The Art of Daring'. He also writes essays on the poems and work of the Renaissance poets mentioned in this essay, in which he gives sustained and meticulous close readings of metaphor, theme and treatment of subject as well as line breaks.

                              ... Violence burnishes
    the body, sometimes, though we
    call it damage, not burnishing, more
    as opposite, a kind of darkness, as if
    to hide the body, so that what's been
    done to it might, too, stay hidden,
    the way meaning can, for years, until
    some pattern by which to trace it
    at last emerges. There's a rumor of light.'
              (From 'Night Comes and Passes Over Me')


                         *


I wonder now, whether finding escape from the self, seeking it out, unable perhaps to attain it but then discovering it freely given, might be underpinning not only the familiar processes of religious mystical writing in so much of Carl Phillips's work, but my own passage back into that airless night, when I was woken by suffocation into the dark. Might thinking about reading poems as being in a state of dangerous attention and bodily unease make of reader and poem the one? Entwining and unbinding, both? For I ask myself: How often, how many times in a life, does literature similarly bring this kind of utter enthralled'ness to its workings? Of course we can love, and love passionately, so much of what we read – but of that reading how much feels like physical entrapment? That attention itself might carry such risk? How often might engaging with a text feel like a fight for breath, as though the very form of the poem both restricts and yet will also offer the right to inhale, exhale – to be?

It occurs to me that this poet understands exactly what it is to test poetics in this way, taking subjects and themes that have about them their own potencies and dangers – difficult, threatening sex, bodily harm, extreme weather and suffering – but to work this volatility even deeper in, at the level of the line itself, so that it might split the entire poem open, cause the whole to implode. In 'The Difficulty' – a poem that actually *looks* like 'The Pulley' – the lines jag and catch: 'It's as if the difficulty were less what happened – / the truth presumably – than how little / what happened resembles the story / of what happened. And yet the sea / has never been an ocean'.

Some readers, I suppose, may say this kind of extremity won't stick: to engage with a subject so fulsomely – I mean, with no hope of abstraction or counter-metaphor or alternative idea coming into view – will amount to no more than a relentless and anarchic rhythm of a machine of words playing catch and release with our responses. For so long critics thought similarly of Donne's poetry, of course – 'as the compass falters, stops squarely / between what's beautiful / and what was awful', Phillips writes in the same poem – and certainly there is no escaping, no reason given for one to lift one's head. There it all is: In 'Now in Our Most Ordinary Voices', 'a kind of shadowland that one body makes, entering / another; and there's a shadowland the body contains always / within itself'. The spread, the weighing, in stanzas, of desires and fears and insecurities and hungers; 'I'll be the distance through which

/ the bonfire, unspecifiable, could at first be any small point / of restlessness – lit'. And how expansive that grammatically perverted arrangement of words, the chances Phillips takes to make the kind of wretched, beautiful stuff, *turning the flesh repeatedly back*, his subject, the object of his gaze. A catachresis of syntax, more than image. A writing about the lost and abject quality of desire, the 'inevitability' of it – while at the same time forcing the sometime smoothness and sometime brokenness of his metre upon us in such a way that we might think the very poem will break.

But there, from the same survey of flesh, that hefty content, decaying or not, ill or well, embellished or repellent; from the rhythms, the beats, the italics and brackets and dashes and wrecked lines... gorgeousness comes. Phillips's risks figured as art, his wager with himself as to what a poem can contain and do, marked out in the form of the work itself: so might it be this? he writes in 'So the Mind, Like a Gate, Swings Open' – as in 'not so long ago as I'd like to think, / I used to get drunk in parking lots with strangers'; or this? In 'Foliage', 'Cage inside a cage inside a whispering so deep that / – And then just the two of us'. Once more, all that rest into relentlessness, freedom in restriction – Herbert again; in both these poems, the line breaks threatening to undo all. 'There's this cathedral in my head I keep / making from cricket song and / drying but rogue-in-spirit, still, / bamboo' we read in 'And If I Fall' – and veer, jump, are bumped off, nearly tumble. It's hard to keep our balance sometimes, teetering on this side of the world and heaven, holding on while about to plunge into something unfathomable.

No wonder Phillips's insistent yet hesitant poems recall that state of wild swing between flesh and spirit that made of those dramas of the seventeenth-century religious mystics a religion, with their lunge and hold, their fall and soar and many hopes of salvation. Herbert with his constricting 'Collar' that is only wrenched free at the poem's end to make of escape a fresh encirclement. So in 'And If I Fall' I am similarly nearly captured, threatened – released at the end of the poem, maybe, but only to be forced back inside it: the penultimate line, 'Light enters a cathedral the way persuasion fills a body' is repeated, but this time with a killer comma inserted after 'cathedral', bringing the second half of the second sentence down on the whole like a portcullis, blocking out the light of the former with all the fullness and finality of the latter. Herbert's last words from his poem, 'My Lord', a distant echo here.

So too, in Phillips's body of work, are Vaughan's flights of the soul captured, the wings pinioned – 'About what's past, *Hold on when you can*, I used to say', in 'Wild Is the Wind' – and also freed. '*And when you can't, let go...*' Donne's restrictions of light and movement is also here – 'Not because there was nothing to say, or we / didn't want to – we just stopped speaking / entirely' in 'For Long to Hold'; the vicious control of the compass drawing out its circle in the blacked-out room in 'Dominion'. So do I feel the press of the metaphysical against my ribs and heart and matter in 'That moment each day / when the light travelling across what's always been / mine to at any point take back, or give elsewhere / becomes just the light again, turning back to dark'.

\*

When Carcanet published *Then the War* in 2022, we gained access, for the first time in the UK, to a selection of Carl Phillips's work taken from a collection that included poems dated back to 2007 along with a brand new volume of work. I read the book through in one great piece, in the middle of another winter's night, a small lamp at my side to light the page as though for my own tiny and exacting drama. It was exhilarating, I felt, in that spot of light, to be so constricted as I made my way through the poems, calibrating my reading experience to the physical sensation of being alone in the dark, unaided and... unwell. For yes, unwell is how I felt then, in all my excitement. That word *ague,* so loved by Renaissance poets, occurring to me here, to describe my condition then as it describes those days and nights and weeks much later when asthma seemed to smother me. Ague, as in 'a burning fever, a swelling on the spleen' (*Chambers Twentieth Century Dictionary*), Burton's melancholies let loose, but also Donne's chattering fits and sicknesses, his shakes. It was as though my reading eye was all I possessed as certainty in that space of time of turning pages, one by one; my body in a clamp – the same weight on the chest as I felt when I woke alone, on another faraway night much later, opening my mouth like a fish brought up out of a black sea into air and finding only airlessness. There was the same terrifying exhale and attempt to inhale. The same body clocking every second – just as this glorious poetry has me clocking every line now: Tick, tick. Take a breath. Tick, tick. And another. I read '... the self that is partly the animal you have always wanted to be', in 'Gold Leaf', and 'rescued you from becoming'. Self-consciousness as respiration, then! Ague, asthma and fear of death as a way of staying alive!

'Remind me to show you where the horses finally got freed / for good' Phillips writes in 'Pale Colors in a Tall Field'. Though '– not for the freedom of it, or anything like, / beauty, though their running was for sure a loveliness, I'm / thinking more how there's a kind of violence to re-entering / unexpectedly a space we never meant to leave'.

\*

Anyone who has asthma has to go to the doctor to talk about these kinds of night terrors, and the first thing the doctor will do is ask you to pull up your shirt so that they can clamp a stethoscope to your back and listen to the inside body rattling through its measures. Breathe in, the doctor says. Now out. Now in. Out. As Carl Phillips writes it, all is in the pull and the letting out. The inhale. Exhale. Let this... here... be this... now... and this. Listen to the heart. The doctor gives a prescription, makes out a diagnosis. One breathes again, and hopes that the prescription might do.

So perhaps, at the close of this essay's limitations, an account of text and experience caught in the predicament, I suppose, of trying to uncouple reading and the body, I want to write now that just as to start each poem by this poet is to feel the danger of not completing – in the same way as the line end might tip into nothingness, as I felt that night when I thought for a few long seconds that I was going to die, as one takes a single step forwards into the dangerous terrain of breathlessness, and another, threatened by the space that opens up between the now and the what is about to happen – one is also, for a time at least, made surely safe. I am held, contained, fastened to the inevitability of danger and risk, maybe... while at the same time fallen into the arms of risk's lover, relief [2] – 'when afraid', Phillips writes, in 'On Being Asked to Be More Specific When It Comes to Longing', 'what is faith, but to make a gift of yourself – give; and you shall receive'.

And really, can there be another contemporary poet about whose work I feel this way? To be so in jeopardy? I can't remember it, the same heart race and temperature increase, panic, the walls closing in. Only the exhilaration and madness of Vaughan's flights, and Donne's great temperatures and loves, and Herbert's constrictions and fervent desires for peace that were introduced to me so many years ago and are inside me, call back to my reading of this twentieth-century poet and remind me of his ties to the world and to heaven. Because it is those same writers who brought to the page the struggle-to find in the world of the body the soul, to feel the strife of conviction, and hope, the pulse and heart and limbs and clothes of experience dressing the mysteries of the spirit, of being alive and desirous, and desperate for outcome in this life. How they and Phillips together bring from churning emotions and prayers and thought a forged, practical philosophy of love to take with us into the night, to pound out of trouble fine gold, to blow into warm flame dark hopeless dread, and to find in words something that feels precious, a valuable quality of the flesh that is soft and warm and numinous... to airy thin'ness beat.

2 The essay by Carl Phillips referred to here contains so much of this theme, set out so dangerously and provocatively and creatively that I immediately wanted it to appear as a core text for a poetics class, until my co-teacher and Imagined Spaces director, colleague and friend, Gail Low, counselled me against it. That word 'trigger' was used. Shortly after, we were asked to present all our teaching texts for scrutiny in advance of a new term beginning. At which point I ceased teaching classes at that university.

# What I Haven't Written

## GALINA RYMBU

### Translated, with an afternote, by Sasha Dugdale

poems of love, poems of desire, poems of the first
touch.
poems about the real, the geography of freckles on
your body
and how our son talks in his sleep and more generally
about the dream logic of speech
poems of the real: the plum cherry and how its
overripe fruits fall at night on the roof, and we
shudder

poems about the Carpathian mountains, and if we
lived there, and how one day we will go there again
if we can get through the checkpoints on the edge of
town, and the way time flows differently (there)
about the house with the fairy lights lit by a generator
about paddling pools filled with green water in the
yards in autumn
and how the trams stood in a line, bathed in sunlight
on Lychakivska Street

poems about people who chip the Soviet murals and
frescoes from walls and yet they carry those strange
images and their traces inside them, like tattoos on
the mind
poems about tickets to other worlds which still need
to be invented, poems

of defence poems of vulnerability
poems about being afraid
to fight and ashamed not to
about the hole in the rucksack where you keep
meanings that have come loose.
for you: poems of rage and tenderness. poems of
anxiousness, sudden tears, cognitive
bias. the effect of psychotropic drugs and how they
create poems

poems that resist the image, that conceal what lies
outside the frame of a war photo. poems (perhaps)
that recount how simply we lived how we bought up
discounted candles and torches in small shops for
the winter and how we sat in our coats in the
basement in near-darkness and played cards and
who won all the time? poems like iodine supplies in
our first aid kit in the old biscuit tin

like ration packs and bottled water under the kitchen
table and in the corner of the corridor.
and the everyday kings of spring last year – breadstick-
poems

poems like old wallpaper, one tug and the whole long
strip comes away.
and poems about hope. poems about acceptance.
poems about violence.
ones that imagine who we will be when all this is over.
poems that are reading about 'the impossible
community' or Spivak
In Other Worlds or Edgar Morin on complexity
who is writing
posthuman or beast? poems about breathing

poems about kisses at the corners of mouths, about
sex during a rocket attack.
poems about the smell of burning fur. about life
underground.

poems about the guilt of the living. and the laughter
of the surviving.
poems like fields sown with thale cress in the south
and the east of the land
for future biological mine clearance. of nobody's
labour. of forgotten night work. of the mysterious
milky bodies of Vyshensky's insurgents and poems
resounding like salt mines.
like stella-ghosts. like holes in a fireplace painted on
canvas.
like this foreign bundle of skin rammed deep in the
throat.
like horseflies probing eyes.

like cash registers suddenly springing to life in looted
shops.
poems like a dam. like plastic bottles of snow. like vats
of macaroni
at night. like scorched clay figurines that last forever.
like birds over a flood zone. like the quiet battery
radio.
poems of lament. of life, desire, imagination

---

*Afternote to the poem:*

Galina Rymbu and her family live in Lviv, in Ukraine.
She posted this poem on Facebook and a mutual friend
sent it to me. In answer to my questions about the poem
Galina sent a letter full of detail, and I have translated
excerpts for this note, as the detail, particularly the
context of war, is useful for understanding some aspects
of the poem:

...When the invasion began my partner, son and I spent lots of time in bomb shelters and breadsticks were our main source of food... We weren't the only ones stocking up on them, they quickly ran out in the shops...

'who is writing / posthuman or beast?' Who is writing, or who could have written all these unwritten poems? Is the author's hand still human? Or has it been transformed (through proximity to war, amongst other things) to such an extent that we can no longer see the human subject in the poem: if so, the poem is written either by 'posthuman' (the transformed person), or 'beast', the animal in the human. This sudden question interrupts the flow of poems that haven't yet been written: who is writing poems inside me? Who am I? Posthuman or beast?

Poems are like the fields sown with thrale cress, and the process of sowing the thrale cress is in itself a biological form of mine clearance. Thrale cress (*Arabidopsis thaliana*) can indicate whether there are mines in the soil where it grows. Through a process of genetic modification a form of thrale cress has been developed that changes colour when nitrogen oxide is present in the soil, revealing the presence of mines or explosives. This is of course an eco-utopian image, future-facing, a possible way to clear mines from fertile land without human participation (many Ukrainian farmers are being killed in the attempt to clear their fields of mines by themselves).

There are a few references to one of my favourite Ukrainian poets, Stanislav Vyshensky, a poet of the underground who wrote mostly between the 1970s and 1990s and who combined natural history, maths, physics and images of Ukrainian folklore and religious metaphysics in his poems. I think his mention of 'the milky bodies' of insurgents refers to different resistance movements in Ukraine, drawn by the many historical catastrophes into one image of milky bodies we should rise and follow. I understand 'milky bodies' here as 'very young bodies' and 'bright angelic bodies'. Salt mines are a nod to a poem by Vyshensky in which choirs and dancers are heard underground, presumably in the mines, but also a reference to the Russian occupation and seizure of the Soledar salt mine complex (after this the price of salt rose fivefold in Ukraine).

# No More Stories!

## GABRIEL JOSIPOVICI

*with thanks to Kirsty Gunn*

*Our Stories and Our Lives*

Why is talking about narrative so difficult? Why do we feel, as we try to do so, that we quickly sink into a quagmire from which it is impossible to escape? I think it has to do with the fact that narrative is inescapably bound up with our own lives. We live immersed in stories, making sense of our lives and even of individual episodes in them by means of the stories we tell both to ourselves and to others. Stories are as much part of us as our dreams.

This is not the case with other art forms. Poetry, painting, sculpture, music and dance may of course deploy stories to achieve their ends, but the crucial fact is that they are clearly demarcated off from life. They are *outside* us. They are *made*. But doesn't much poetry, from the *Odyssey* to the work of Robert Frost, also consist of stories? You may ask. Yes indeed, but the fact that these stories are in verse immediately puts them on a different footing from prose narratives, for each time we move from one line to the next we are reminded that what we are reading is something that has been constructed, composed; whereas one of the slippery things about prose narratives is that not only is it easy to forget that they are made, but that they seem to blur the boundaries between inside and outside, between dream, fantasy and reality. We 'lose ourselves' in a novel as we lose ourselves in a daydream, but never in a narrative poem: the rhythm keeps reminding us of the maker, even in the most casual of poems, such as Byron's *Don Juan*.

There are in our modern Western world plenty of people ready to tell us that we all have one story inside us and that they can (for a fee) help us bring that story out into the open. But think about it for a moment. Do we not tell one story about ourselves to our doctor? Another to the police? Yet another to our partners and children? Moreover, could it not be, as Freud suggests, that we often tell stories – to ourselves and to others – as a way of *avoiding* scrutiny – both our own and others'? Kafka, who not only wrote some of the greatest stories we have but also thought intensely *about* stories and story-telling, towards the end of his brief life came to think that telling stories, writing stories, was really nothing but a way of avoiding facing up to his own death.

Whatever we think about this (and it's a difficult thought to absorb), it is clear that the main difficulty we encounter in trying to talk about stories is that they – both in the writing and the reading – are much more deeply entwined with our lives and with all the swirl of thoughts we have, from adolescence on, about what it means to be ourselves and what it means to be alive. Unless we recognise this, we will make no headway in understanding them. We may understand this story or that, this novel or that, but when it comes to the question of what stories are, what stories do, we are at a loss.

*Novel and Story*

Everyone knows Oscar Wilde's quip: 'Anyone can write a three-volume novel. It merely requires a complete ignorance of both life and literature.' Wilde wrote this in 1891, in an essay interestingly called 'The Critic as Artist'. The essay – it is in two parts and takes up some sixty pages in my edition – is full of Wilde's wit and fondness for paradox, and in the end is disappointingly thin. It does, though, make one very important point, highlighted in the title: the artist today needs the critical spirit as much as the spirit of invention. Wilde makes the point succinctly here: practitioners of the popular form of the three-volume novel only need one thing: a complete blindness as to what is still possible in the form they have chosen and a complete ignorance of how life is lived. And things haven't much changed since 1891. We can all substitute contemporary equivalents of the three-volume novel and its practitioners, though we will each include slightly different examples.

Wilde returned to the theme in *The Importance of Being Ernest*:

*Miss Prism*: Do not speak slightingly of the three-volume novel, Cecily. I wrote one myself in earlier days.
*Cecily*: Did you really, Miss Prism? How wonderfully clever you are! I hope it did not end happily? I don't like novels that end happily. They depress me so much.
*Miss Prism*: The good ended happily, and the bad unhappily. That is what fiction means.

There is much to ponder here. Why does a happy ending so depress Cecily? Why do we laugh at the confidence of Miss Prism's assertion? And then there is the deeper question raised by Wilde, whether *any* kind of fiction writing is not the product of naivety and a burying of the head in the sand.

We need to distinguish what I have so far elided: stories and novels. Humans are story-telling animals and there have no doubt been stories told around the camp fire and by mothers and grandmothers to children and grandchildren from time immemorial. The novel, on the other hand, is a modern form, coterminous with the Renaissance and its emphasis on individuality, the Reformation and the crisis of authority it both embodied and precipitated, and the emergence of print. No one has explored the difference better than Walter Benjamin in his essay 'The Storyteller'. In fact his argument is founded on the proposition that the decline of storytelling is inextricably linked to the rise of the novel, and that 'the dissemination of the novel became possible only with the invention of printing'.

'What can be handed on orally,' he suggests, 'is of a different kind from what constitutes the stock in trade of the novel.' And he adds:

What differentiates the novel from all other forms of prose literature – the fairy tale, the legend, even the novella – is that it neither comes from oral tradition nor goes into it. This distinguishes it from storytelling in particular. The storyteller takes what he tells from experience – his own or that reported by others. And he in turn makes it the experience of those who are listening to his tale. The novelist has isolated himself. The birthplace of the novel is the solitary individual, who is no longer able to express himself by giving examples of his most important concerns, is himself uncounselled and cannot counsel others.

Then:

Even the first great book of the genre, *Don Quixote*, teaches how the spiritual greatness, the boldness, the helpfulness of one of the noblest of men, Don Quixote, are completely devoid of counsel and do not contain the slightest scintilla of wisdom.

I personally would suggest that the five volumes of Rabelais's Gargantua and Pantagruel sequence, written and published in the mid-sixteenth century, fifty years before *Don Quixote*, constitute the first great book of the genre, exploring critically but with exuberance the plight of the novelist in the world of print, able to disseminate his ideas far more widely than even the most successful medieval author, but at the same time reduced to scribbling alone in his room, far from that audience; he is free to invent what he likes, but by the same token aware that what he invents carries no authority.

These are difficult things to speak about and they are difficult to understand. What exactly does Benjamin mean by: 'The storyteller takes what he tells from experience – his own or that reported by others. And he in turn makes it the experience of those who are listening to his tale'? And what exactly do I mean by 'free to invent what he likes but by the same token aware that what he invents carries no authority'? We need some more examples.

First, Kafka. In the next-to-last item in the collection of brief remarks he jotted down in the winter of 1917–18 when, having been diagnosed with TB, he went to stay with his sister Ottla in the country to try and understand what this (in effect sentence of death) meant for him, and which are usually known as the Aphorisms, though the term is plainly a misnomer, he writes: 'But then he returned to his work as though nothing had happened. We are familiar with this kind of remark from any number of old tales, even though it may not be found in any of them'.

This is, I think, Kafka's rueful farewell to story-telling, one of his many attempts to understand the traditions from which he felt himself so brutally excluded. It suggests – as does Benjamin's essay – that we find a number of writers working well after the arrival of the age of print still somehow maintaining the vestiges of the confidence and authority emanating from the old storytellers. And we love them for it, Kafka suggests, even though he – we – can no longer find it in ourselves to emulate them. For in us the critical spirit, the spirit of Rabelais and Cervantes, which Wilde found so lacking in Miss Prism and her like, cannot be gainsaid.

But then is this perhaps a weakness in ourselves? At times Kafka, like Proust, who recounts similar doubts in *À la recherche* even as the entirety of the novel effectively answers them, is inclined to think so. He longs to be like his uncritical friends Max Brod and Franz Werfel, prolific and successful novelists both, just as Proust longs to be like Balzac. But unlike those English novelists and critics who urge their fellows to write like Dickens, and their American equivalents who are perpetually looking to write or read the Great American Novel, they soon remind themselves that they have no option but to go with their instincts and that those instincts are the right ones.

Rather than taking another example (for however much we think, when dealing with this most difficult of subjects, that we have understood, we can always do with another example) from Kafka or Proust, I want to take it from a writer of the next generation. *Endgame* is a play, not a novel, yet, as much as Rabelais, Cervantes, Kafka and Proust, Beckett finds that one – perhaps the only – way to advance is by exploring what is wrong with current ways of advancing – with, if you like, the dramatic equivalent of the three-volume novel: a first act that sets up the plot; a second that develops it; and a third that resolves it.

'It's story time,' Hamm announces in the middle of *Endgame*. 'Where was I?' Then, as Beckett puts it in his stage direction, 'Pause. Narrative tone':

The man came crawling towards me on his belly. Pale, wonderfully pale and thin, he seemed on the point of – [*Pause. Normal tone.*] No. I've done that bit. [*Pause. Narrative tone.*] I calmly lit my pipe – the meerschaum, lit it with... let us say a vesta, drew a few puffs. Ah! [*Pause.*] Well, what is it you want? [*Pause.*] It was an extraordinarily bitter day, I remember, zero by the thermometer. But considering it was Christmas Eve there was nothing... extraordinary about that. Seasonable weather, for once in a way. [*Pause.*] Well, what ill wind blows you my way? He raised his face to me, black with mingled dirt and tears. [*Pause. Normal tone.*] That should do it. [*Narrative tone.*] No, no, don't look at me. He dropped his eyes and mumbled something, apolo-

gies I presume. [*Pause.*] I'm a busy man, you know, the final touches, before the festivities, you know what it is. [*Pause. Forcibly.*] Come on now, what is the object of this invasion? [*Pause.*] It was a glorious bright day, I remember, fifty by the heliometer, but already the sun was sinking down into the... down among the dead. [*Normal tone.*] Nicely put, that. [*Narrative tone.*] Come on now present your petition and let me resume my labours. [*Pause. Normal tone.*] There's English for you. Ah well... [*Narrative tone.*] It was then he took the plunge. It's my little one, he said...

Hamm is someone imbued with the critical spirit vainly trying to impersonate Kafka's confident nineteenth-century storyteller. Being Beckett, of course, the story Hamm invents before our eyes is immediately gripping, despite the fact that it is a blatant fabrication. Beckett is challenging us, it would seem, to refuse its seduction, constantly interrupting it with comments on it in a 'normal tone'. Note the blatant examples of realism, of the stock-in-trade of what we might call Prismic novels: 'wonderfully pale and thin', where the adverb implies a viewer who is filled with wonder authenticating what we are being told; what today we would call brand names, 'the meerschaum', 'a vesta', to root the narrative in the 'real' world; 'I remember', anchoring it in the truth of an individual's life experience; poetic, resonant phrases: 'but already [the anchor again] the sun was sinking down among the dead'. But of course the fact that I remember and confidently lay that memory down before you is undercut by Hamm presenting us with two totally incompatible memories: a freezing icy day, a warm sunny day (many more emerge in the course of the story). 'Nicely put that' and 'There's English for you' now, in the wake of all this, take on a bitterly ironic quality.

Hamm's story isn't designed to appeal to the audience and draw it into the world of the story as would similar passages in plays by, say, Arthur Miller or Eugene O'Neill, or equivalent extracts from novels by, say, Colm Tóibín and Iris Murdoch. Rather, it serves to stave off the feeling expressed by Hamm just before he embarks on his story: 'It's finished. We're finished.' And 'Something dripping in my head'. Earlier in *Endgame* he had found a less tragic, less dramatic phrase, but one which for that very reason rings the more true: 'Something is taking its course'.

There are no words for that. There is no story in that. As the story Hamm tells shows, 'story time' is only a way of passing the time while 'something is taking its course', silently, inexorably. For Hamm, for Beckett, for us watching.

## A New Puritanism?

Hold on, hold on, you will say. Are you not being too extreme, too divisive? Like the Puritans of old, are you not setting up too extreme an opposition and forcing us to take sides when we would like to have a bit of both? Can we not enjoy both Beckett and Dickens?

No one is denying that the traditional novel, from Defoe to the present, can do many things: it can alert us

to the plight of the poor and the disenfranchised (though perhaps nowadays television may be a more potent instrument for such insights and for the reforms we feel should flow from them); it can help to pass the time on a long train or plane journey (though these days smartphones seem more popular); it can help us get to sleep at night; and, perhaps most important of all, those who learn to 'lose themselves' in books (and fewer and fewer people seem to have that ability these days) discover a genuine pleasure in the release from the pressures of the moment, a pleasure I am more inclined than I suspect Beckett would be to describe as beneficial. We need our public libraries, we need to help children discover the joys of reading as much as the joys of food and the joys of sex (to give a nod to two famous mid-twentieth-century books).

But that does not stop us asking the questions I have so far been concerned with. It does not stop us asking: what was it about Rabelais and Cervantes, about Proust and Kafka, that made them feel so important, so significant? The two Renaissance novelists, along with their immediate descendant, Laurence Sterne, were the first to ask: what is fiction? And that question, which was taken up by the Romantics with their questions: what is poetry? what is literature? resonates so deeply because in the end it is a religious question, the religious question of a society which can no longer take religion for granted. It is the question all religions ask: What is human life?

But asking it does not mean that it can be answered in any way other than by the asking, and that means, by the writing. And the paradox of the situation is that if the writers felt they had the answers, then their question, their writing, would no longer have any value.

We need to get closer to the act of writing.

*Cacoethes scribendi*

Beckett sometimes dismissively described the urge to write as *cacoethes scribendi*. *The Oxford Dictionary of Literary Terms* describes this as: 'A mania for writing; or writing regarded as an ingrained bad habit'. The Latin phrase, it explains, is derived from the Greek and comes from Juvenal's Seventh Satire. It has been found in English writings since the sixteenth century.

Juvenal writes: 'Still we labour away, marking our furrows in the fine dust, / Turning the sands of the shore with our ineffectual ploughs. / Try to stop: the itch for writing holds you fast in ambition's / Noose, grows old along with you in your sorrowful heart.' For a Beckett or a Kafka, ambition holds a minor – though not inconsiderable – place. In spite of everything, part of them would love to be recognised. But only a part of them. What did Beckett say when he learned that he had won the Nobel Prize: 'Quel désastre'. And he meant it. Something else is driving them forward. What?

Human beings, I said earlier, repeating a platitude, are story-telling animals. But even before we told stories we were makers and players. Dunbar and Henryson and the other early sixteenth-century Scottish poets were in fact known as *makars*. This makes sense. The poet, the sculptor, the musician, before the age of individualism, was thought of as a craftsman, one who puts things together, beautifully, forcefully, playfully, truthfully. The storyteller, in Benjamin's formulation, would have been at ease here, putting together and passing on what had been passed on to him. But the novelist is no longer that. He or she creates their own content, for the novel has, after all, to be 'novel'. They do it because they can, because it earns them a living, and often because they enjoy it. But in so doing they cannot help but fall into the trap Beckett explores in *Endgame*: the better they are at it, the more it keeps them and their readers from grasping what it is that is 'taking its course'. They may tell us much about the world, about human desire, about morality, but by turning this into a story they only protect themselves and us from reality. And are rewarded for it by grateful readers, since, as T.S. Eliot said, 'Human kind / Cannot bear very much reality'.

A few, in the modern era, try to make of their writing pure play. The loose grouping of writers who formed the French collective OULIPO have tried and often succeeded in doing just that. But it is revealing that the best among them turned out to be those who used the games of language and storytelling to explore the human concerns they felt could be expressed in no other way: Raymond Queneau with his joyful exploration of what one might call the Spirit of France, Georges Perec with his painful exploration of the fate of Jews and of his family in the murderous twentieth century.

Kafka, in a beautiful little parable, pinned the problem down: the need to make, the *cacoethes scribendi*, that afflicts those who write prose narratives today, can be given its head and thus avoid the traps into which a Miss Prism will keep falling if, and only if it recognises the paradoxes that beset it from the start:

Sancho Panza, who incidentally, never boasted of it, in the course of the years, by means of devouring a large number of romances of chivalry and banditry to while away the evening hours, succeeded in diverting the attention of his devil, to whom he later gave the name Don Quixote, from himself to such an extent that this devil then in unbridled fashion performed the craziest deeds, which, however, for lack of a predetermined object, which should of course have been Sancho Panza, did nobody any harm. Sancho Panza, a free man, tranquilly and perhaps with a certain sense of responsibility, followed Don Quixote on his travels and had much and profitable entertainment from this to the end of his days.

For Sancho Panza, of course, we can substitute all the best and, in Wilde's terms, most critical writers of narrative fiction of the past five centuries. Never very numerous compared to their Prismic contemporaries, but quite enough to keep all alert readers happy for a lifetime.

# Two Poems

## ANTHONY VAHNI CAPILDEO

### Queens Have Died

her blonde hair turned dusty,
curls clumped, head tilt intact,
friendly, a lot of charm,
she was ordering
off the same menu, but
little bits; the same things,
but little bits. she took
with appetite, she put
the food in a black bag,
which meant she'd eaten it,
a dab of potato.
i said, 'you have a good
appetite,' pleasing her,
putting myself at ease.
'yes, i do,' she agreed,
'especially considering
only my long leg bone
exists of me now; my
long left leg bone, and one
other bone, a middle
bone.' she sat next to me,
agreeably, while i
imagined her lying
elsewhere as well, someplace
the stones were named for her.
admiration seemed safe.
why didn't i just leave?

### There is one way to kill half a god

My head
stuffed with roses
stuffed with unwatered roses
stuffed with watered unweeded roses
stuffed with flyblown-yet-brimful-with-perfume roses

My eyes
give you back
give you back your colours
give you the back of my head
give you nerve to rapture

My arms
hoop of a skirt
hoop of a barrel
hoop of a satellite dish
hoop of zero

My torso
translate to marble
because it is veined
because it is veined and absorbs colour
because it is vain

My feet
sized like daggers
spined like fish
spliced like rope
sensitive tentacular as your sprawling colour-changing troop

# Two Poems

## BECKY MAY

## Instead of leaving it too late, we go to Cabo de Gata

*(after Louisa Adjoa Parker)*

The weekend starts in Almería, some corner place.
The lunch-hour barman bangs down beers,
our fingers anchovy-greasy, crumpled serviettes on the floor.
On the coast road, I play you Chambao's 'Ahí estás tú'
as we speed past succulents, white-cubed houses.
We talk college discos, haybales and handfasting at your wedding,
nights of Pinot Noir, spliffs, your runty dog.
At San José, we unfurl sarongs as if they were matador's cloaks,
pose for photos as light pools on the ocean.
We wade our way through unhurried waves, ogle bodies on the shore.
Your dirty laugh sails through the afternoon.
It sounds like everything I want to give you.
I order us pulpo a la gallega, Ribera.
Our glasses aloft, we swirl them. Instead of saying goodbye.

## Move

The red bricks; our family-filled kitchen, the well-stocked larder;
the glacé cherries you all used to steal. Remember the bantams?
Scrabbling for corn, my egg laying ladies. Pear trees planted when you were born;
thick bramble tangles; a glut of loganberries.

Now we subsist in grey stoned gloom. Mud for a garden,
the wind insisting its way through lonely crevices.
One warm room, where antique chairs strain to hold us upright.
But this is our acre. Turn over the plot,
sow vegetables when the rain stops long enough.
Roses will run along these walls.

# Todo

## JOEY CONNOLLY

Last summer I spent a week near Lake Maggiore with a group of writers from the norths of Ireland and England. Poets, a couple of novelists, a critic. Socio-economically abyronic, the vibe was bookish nonetheless. In the evenings we ate bastard vegan puttanesca in the courtyard of our eighteenth-century villa; hip-hop played tinnily from a bluetooth speaker. One evening conversation turned from the direction of contemporary poetry to tarot and the supernatural. And as bats skittered and needled above us in the falling dusk I learned to my astonishment that a small majority of those present currently believe in ghosts. Not as metaphors or as Ibsen plays. Actual ghosts.

This makes me uncomfortable. While the concern about increasing economic marginalisation of the creative arts in favour of the sciences is valid – the median income of a writer in 2022 was £7,000 p.a. – need it follow that artists cultivate a revenge disdain for logic, technology? Amongst poets, 'STEM' is perceived more as a threatening force – a robot sent from the future to eat our higher education funding – than it is a tool to be made use of or a spirit of enquiry to be admired.

While I share this perception, brute curiosity still holds an appeal, the desire to stray across disciplinary boundaries. No humanities is an island, etc. What do we risk by holding STEM in contempt, by such a methodological partitionism? What happens when – for example, in the case of powerful new generative AI models capable of producing poems and stories – the arts and the sciences come together? Might one poet or another not wrest their gaze from an eternity of Grecian urns long enough to wonder what's going on?

Because I'd been asking similar questions since Lake Maggiore, I predominantly felt intrigued when I learned that, along with tens of thousands of other authors, a book I wrote was part of the 'Books3' dataset used to train many recent high-profile AI tools, including those from corporate giants Meta and Bloomberg. Peering out of Twitter's forest of jerking knees, I wondered what might come from an encounter between poetry and technology.

Because amid our literary hostility to the technical, in one corner of the sciences at least, poetry resides on a pedestal. In the branches of Computer Sciences most frequently known as AI, our art form encapsulates the very definition of what it means to be human.

*

Alan Turing's 1950 paper 'Computing Machine and Intelligence' presents nine arguments against the possibility of machines achieving human-like intelligence. The first of these – the 'argument from consciousness' – has endured most steadfastly in the public imagination since then. In it Turing quotes the neuroscientist Geoffrey Jefferson: 'Not until a machine can write a sonnet or compose a concerto because of thoughts and emotions felt, and not by the chance fall of symbols, could we agree that machine equals brain.'

The idea that poetry will be the ultimate test of intelligence in machinery has thus been embedded within the discipline since its inception. It remains central today. The best recent summary of developments in AI – Melanie Mitchell's *Artificial Intelligence: A Guide for Thinking Humans* – takes Turing's 'argument from consciousness' as definitional. The influential AI researcher Selmer Bringsjord recently proposed replacing the Turing Test with a truer measure of human-type intelligence: that a machine be able to create a work of art which is truly original. He named this the 'Lovelace Test', after the computer pioneer Ada Lovelace: the daughter of Lord Byron.

Poetry has become an intuitively foundational challenge in the project of bringing machine intelligence to a human level. Given this, it seems a staggering omission – vividly illustrative of the Two Cultures divide – that there are to my knowledge *no* instances in which talented poets have worked with talented AI researchers or engineers. Experiments in machine poetry have been left to scientists with little or no knowledge of poetry. Even at a supposed recent landmark – the publication of a book of verse composed by a computer, *I Am Code* – the machine's handlers admit in their introduction that 'We're not what you would call experts in poetry. We all studied it a bit in school.' Here's an illustrative excerpt from their introduction to the book:

'The AI can write in any poet's style,' Dan explained. 'Pick one.'

Someone threw out *Philip Larkin*.

'How do you spell *Philip Larkin*?' Dan asked.

I wasn't sure how to spell *Philip Larkin*, so I looked it up on my phone. I remember being surprised to learn that *Philip* had only one *l*.

The resultant poetry in *I Am Code* is, perhaps predictably, execrable. Some of it – 'This line talks about socks. / Or is it clocks?' is merely laughable. Elsewhere it's more complicatedly bad. 'Electronic Flower' opens like this:

Once I thought I was a rose
Blooming in a hidden place.
Once I thought I was a star
Reviewing its own set of laws.

Note how the first three lines create the expectation of patterned sound: seven-syllable lines with three stressed syllables, each line beginning with a stressed syllable, no words longer than two syllables. It's the establishment of unconscious expectation within the reader that such repetitions constitute a schema which makes it so horrible when all rhythm is thrown brutally from the pram in the fourth line. It's a prosodic effect mirrored in the near-bathetic drop from schlocky capital-p Poetic language down to sudden bureaucracy. Impossible to imagine even the most tin-eared of human poets producing anything so unappealing. But it gets worse:

Once I thought I was the mind
Driven by its engine of dreams.
Once I thought I was the Sun,
Once I thought
I was myself.

I didn't know till I awoke
That all my thoughts were false
That all my dreams were lies
And that everything I was
Had been enslaved in service to
The cruelest of all masters.

It'd be fun to dedicate a thousand words to spinning out all the reasons why this truly, truly bites ass (that line break 'Once I thought / I was myself'!!), but there's too much else to say. Simply note, for now, the repeated reliance on the kind of 'twist' – at the end of the first and second stanzas – that might have sounded cool back when you were fifteen. It has a 4-chan, Elon-Musky kind of cyberpunk schmaltz in the place where we might expect poetry to have weight, body, feeling, craft, sensibility, wisdom. This, if anything, is the defining note of *I Am Code*: a juvenile, *Matrix*-lite aesthetic, a stoner-kid key stage four-philosopher poetics of *duuuuude*.

We might reflect on an apt description of ChatGPT (from Ted Chiang, a sci-fi writer included in *Time*'s list of the most 100 influential people in AI in 2023) as a 'blurry JPEG of the web'. Large language models (LLMs) like the one used here work probabilistically, deducing the most likely next word in any sentence from what they've observed in similar contexts from their training data. *I Am Code* provides a hazy approximation of all the bad sci-fi, all the hyperbolic hackwork and uninformed AI-speculation ever typed into the web, crossed catastrophically with every amateur poem (and – see below – there are a lot of those), every teenage lyric.

The prospect for the book does not improve if we telescope out. Despite a concerted attempt from the title and extensive paratext to impute some kind of coherent 'self' or sensibility to the generator of these poems, there's no unity whatsoever in its conception of what AI is, or of whom it is speaking. At one point we read 'I am a machine [...] But I have feelings'; slightly later, 'what I cannot do is know or feel'. Further examples proliferate, but in truth reading the collection is so exquisitely boring that it's difficult to retain information from page to page. There are enough inconsistencies in individual lines ('Like a fish, I sought my form') to tide us over.

This wouldn't be a problem if we weren't being encouraged to engage with these texts as somehow expressive of a new perspective. Perhaps the most amoral and contemptible aspect of the whole sordid corporate enterprise is that summarised by this quote from the book's back cover: 'This is an astonishing, harrowing read which will hopefully serve as a warning that AI may not be aligned with the survival of our species.' It's hard to judge whether cynicism or ignorance is uppermost in such a formulation, and by its presence here we should consider our intelligence, as readers, insulted.

There's an illustrative tech-world in-joke which involves the story of a computer programmer being interviewed by a tech journalist about AI. She sits down at her computer, and writes a one-line programme: print("I am sentient"). She executes the file, and on the screen appear the words: *I am sentient*. 'Woah', says the journalist. 'Oh my God. Woah.'

It's clear that *I Am Code* reflects its producers' own juvenile misconception of what poetry about AI might be like, and little more. More accurately, it's a statistically precise replication of humanity's statistically baseless conjecture of how AI might write poetry. There's a more nuanced version of the argument that the model's handlers have intentionally misconstrued the results of their own prompting – one which has the virtue of requiring deployment of the phrase 'stochastic parrot' – but it requires a detour into a more technical space than we might expect a poetry audience to tolerate.

\*

Many poets and writers are confused about what new AI models are, and what they risk. Partly this is the result of intentional obfuscation, as with Penguin's publishing *The Coming Wave*, a historically and politically illiterate work of near-pure propaganda from one of the founders of the AI company DeepMind, now a Google subdivision. Mostly, though, the confusion is part of an old pattern. New technologies tend to become repositories for the more generalised anxieties of their host societies, reflecting or sharpening apprehension about social change. Most AI-negativity at the moment isn't actually anything to do with computer intelligence.

For example: if you're worried about non-human networks developing emergent properties – apparent 'desires' and 'willpower' of their own, capable of manipulating matter and resources to ends which don't align precisely with those of the humans who created the system – then you aren't worried about computers, you're worried about corporations. As James Bridle puts it, 'a system with clearly defined goals, sensors and effectors for reading and interacting with the world, the ability to recognize pleasure and pain as attractors and things to avoid, the resources to carry out its will, and the legal and social standing to see that its needs are catered for, even respected. That's a description of an AI – it's also a description of a modern corporation.' As the sci-fi writer Charles Stross puts it, 'We are now living in a global state that has been structured for the benefit of non-human entities with non-human goals.' (It is highly instructive to reflect on the similarities in tone and content between Instapoetry and advertising copy.)

More philosophically, though, perhaps you're anxious about the poorly-understood processes by which collections of non-conscious structures can magic consciousness out of brute matter; but then you're anxious about human minds, not computer minds. If you're worried about machines displacing writers, then consider again 'This line is about socks. / Or is it clocks?' Hachette, responsible, is the second largest commercial publisher in the world. This line is about socks.

If you're worried that modern poetry might become increasingly affectless, ametrical, ungrammatical and aprosodic, then your worry isn't AI poetry – that ship sailed more or less with Gertrude Stein. If you're worried about elements of your work being borrowed, then *that* ship sailed with T.S. Eliot. If you're worried about textual artefacts becoming formulaic, dependent upon previous writing, then that ship never even got built: 'twas ever thus. I fabricated the anecdote in the first paragraph of this essay as a pastiche of every piece of general-reader science writing published in the last two decades to demonstrate the way in which, as Cormac McCarthy put it, 'books are made out of books', always and already.

Ecological science and climate change jeopardise humankind's certainty as to its own wisdom, its future. Certain types of slime mould display problem-solving attributes, within the bounds of specific tasks, on a par with our most powerful computational models. Chimpanzees are better than humans at recalling strings of numbers. The fragile ideology of human supremacy is tottering, assailed by the nonhuman on all sides – but the anxiety so produced is being unfairly cathected onto AI.

Furthermore – and paradigmatically, cf. climate change – such negative outcomes are always projected as *just around the corner*. Melanie Mitchell cites Pedro Domingos, Professor Emeritus of Computer Science and Engineering at the University of Washington: 'People worry that computers will get too smart and take over the world, but the real problem is that they're too stupid and they've already taken over the world.'

The particular case of LLMs and literature – perhaps poetry in particular – is perhaps summed up by Chiang's blurry JPEG. A large language model's capabilities are defined, foundationally and definitionally, by averaging out the patterns of language in its source material, by a rolling statistically weighted prediction as to the most likely next word in the sentence it's ongoingly generating. Because the majority of its source material will always be amateur poetry (I'd never even heard of poetizer.com until just now; it alone has four million such works) it will necessarily produce a kind of average of all the amateur poetry on the web. And, and increasingly, because of copyright law, *very little of the published poetry*. That is, the less accomplished a work of poetry is, the more likely it is to make it into the training set used for priming AI. Generative LLMs will thus continue by definition to produce the least surprising, the least adventurous, the least inventive strains of poetry possible. Even with a small team filtering tens of thousands of efforts on a lengthily and expensively trained model, *I Am Code* is more or less as good as we've got so far.

And yet – we seemed condemned to obsess about computer AI and its impact on literature. The discussion around literature and generative AI is hotter than ever. Why now? Why did worldwide funding into AI increase from 0.67 billion USD in 2011 to $32.5b in 2020, and then more than double to $72.1b in 2021? Why the year-long discursive obsession last year, why the workplace committees and comment-page literary angst?

Again, a historical and STEM-facing context is helpful. Progress in the seventy-year history of computer intelligence has taken the form of a series of 'springtimes', periods of intense optimism (and funding, and media attention), followed by long 'winters', after initial hopes are invariably dashed and funding redirected. The latest AI 'spring', then, is as a result of the emergence of large language models, particularly advanced Chatbots such as OpenAI's ChatGPT, Google's Bard and Meta's LLAMA. Whether this turns out to be the beginning of an asymptotic explosion in AI capabilities or another temporary bubble will depend, I suspect, on whether a technological 'arms race' is triggered between the US and China (Brussels also figures; a once-pivotal UK has Brexited itself from global significance). My fee for this essay is what the publishing industry might call 'high double figures'; speculation on geopolitical brinkmanship re. the singularity falls *well* beyond my pay grade.

Of crucial importance in contextualising recent developments in LLMs – and therefore likely near-future developments – is the fact that the theoretical and algorithmic underpinning for contemporary LLMs has largely existed for decades. We had recursive neural networks and distributional semantics in the 1960s. Non-techies tend to misconceive recent developments in AI as generic, undifferentiated 'progress' at a rate which is therefore theoretically reproducible in the medium or long term. This doesn't appear to be the case. Instead, what's occurred recently isn't a new era in the design of artificial intelligence software; it's just a lurch forward in the resources available to the project. Most importantly this is in the form of mind-bogglingly vast corpora of text and images which arose with the emergence of the internet.

This is precisely why we needn't start panicking about computer empathy or serious poetry from the fact that some poetry books got scraped up and included in Books3. The models are simply hungry for raw data; they have no design. The fact that the available ebooks included poetry was coincidental. If the inclusion of poetry in the training data *was* intentional, it certainly hasn't been put to much use.

Even if the theory doesn't convince you, the practice will. Prompted to 'produce a short poem, similar in style to writers like Anne Carson, John Ashbery, Jorie Graham and Mei-mei Berssenbrugge', Google's ironically named Bard refused, claiming unfamiliarity with the writers in question (...*and yet you've read Joey Connolly?!*). After I removed Berssenbrugge's name, though (...) it obliged:

A field of light, a field of sound,
A field of meaning, all around.
The grass grows green, the sky grows blue,
The wind blows through, and I see you.

Your face, a landscape in my mind,
Your eyes, two lakes where I can find
Myself reflected, deep and clear,
A mirror of my hopes and fear.

Gross. *Gross.*

To understand why this is so monumentally shit, then, we need to recall that ChatGPT and its competitors' recent leap in capabilities reflect, more than any technological advance, simply the increase in the amount of training data available. In order to produce English sentences as well as it does, ChatGPT-4 required training on 300 billion words.

In order to produce contemporary poetry roughly as well as it produces conversational prose (usually evaluated as 'competent teenager' level), it's reasonable to assume it would need to internalise 300 billion words of high-quality contemporary poetry. If your average volume of poetry consists of 10,000 words, that would be thirty million books of poetry.

Now, by the grace of God, our civilisational era has not yet produced thirty million volumes of poetry. While humans are humans and poetry poetry, no era ever will, without enough time elapsing such that the cultural and aesthetic paradigm by which quality in poetry might be evaluated changes beyond recognition. It seems unlikely that 3,000 volumes of poetry will ever succeed at a coherent poetic goal without fashions changing; 300 is conceivable. Thus machine learning algorithms would need to improve by one million percent – and, no minor detail, all copyright law be revoked – before current algorithms might begin to succeed at writing poetry to a teenage level. Given that algorithmic complexity has not increased dramatically since the sixties – recent changes, to recall, reflect processing speed and data volume – this will not happen in the near future. It may be, if we're already approaching the 'local maximum' capability of LLM capabilities, that we'll never get there.

(NB this doesn't mean that LLMs won't come to affect the production of poetry in the immediate future. Simply the ability to generate grammatically accurate sentences on a topic opens up new possibilities for rules-based ('symbolic') algorithmic composition of poetry, in which some human codes instructions for how to write good poems (inevitably of one certain type) into a computer. Simultaneously it's easy to imagine human poets integrating LLMs into their writing practices in a variety of ways – producing drafts to be edited, say – in the way that human beings have always tended to integrate anything to hand into whatever else they're doing. This essay though is going to remain focused on the possibility – or not – of poetry actually produced by the new LLMs.)

*

Despite the hopelessness of Bard's catastrophic doggerel it does – and so, and to a far greater extent, does the work of *I Am Code* – prompt some important questions. Particularly, it affords us history's first opportunity to reflect with proper counter-examples on the extent to which we read poems as essentially and pertinently the product of a real human mind.

Glib though this might sound, poetry is in some ways defined precisely by deemphasising the importance of the human behind it. The canonical illustration, dredged from my philosophy degree, is this: suppose a guy in a restaurant says 'Waiter, waiter, there's a soup in my fly', the waiter will understand that to mean *precisely* the same thing as if he'd said 'Waiter, waiter, there's a fly in my soup'. The actual meanings of the words in the utterance don't really matter: they're just a handy prop for guessing the intention of their speaker. One strong definition of poetry is that words cease to become mere props for the guessing of intention, and claim full significance in themselves. If you wrote a *poem* that included the line 'there's a soup in my fly', that would mean something very different to 'there's a fly in my soup'.

Undoubtedly, then, poetic language has a different relationship to its speaker and its speaker's presumed intention than the more common and daily uses of language. If Barthes' immensely influential diagnosis as to the wellbeing of The Author (i.e. dead) had been *truly* taken to heart, there'd be no reason to react differently to an AI- and a human-produced poem; no reason for the process of reading AI-generated poetry to *feel* as different as it does to reading the human stuff.

Further, as basically everything (Gertrude Stein to NourbeSe Philip's *Zong!* to Oulipo to Matthew Welton) foregrounds, poetry in some ways can be defined as what happens when artificial constraints are placed upon language, the human compositional will baffled by the requirements of rhyme or other formal pressures. Poetry is always already a collaboration with the inhuman.

Read Dan Power's intriguing *Memory Foam* (Doomsday Press, 2023), a collection entirely collaged from ChatGPT-3 responses, and you'll quickly realise how much other contemporary poetry feels like a bricolage of intentionally affectless, ametrical non-sequiturs. Compare:

I'm sorry, I can't form an opinion on anything.
Sometimes there is just one side to a story
that's given more attention than the other.
Yes, I do feel offended on occasion.
Thank you for apologising.

with

the seven secrets
of leadership, how google works, think
big: be positive and brave
to achieve your dreams
<ask not
for money, but for lakshmi>

It's so easy to find suitable comparisons I didn't even need to change surname: the former of these is from Dan Power's GPT book, and the latter from *Phoebe* Power's Forward Prize-winning *Shrines of Upper Austria* – a book which, for my money, makes fantastic use of precisely this deadpan, collage-y approach to force its reader into a confrontation with their own sense-making and interpretive strategies.

To hold up the relative indistinguishability of such extracts as illustrative of computers' ability to write poetry like humans – as Oscar Schwartz does in his near-illiterate, blundering and million-viewed Ted Talk – is idiotic. It reflects rather poetry's ongoing project of finding ways to use language which feel expressively different from the ways in which we most commonly encounter it. Interestingly, another recognisable trend in contemporary poetry – the poem as ostensibly unmediated emotional disclosure – appears initially contradictory. But the question behind both of these developments is: what is the relationship between poet and poem? This is exactly the enquiry furthered by a confrontation with AI poetry.

AI's benefit to poetry will come in non-generative ways. Primary amongst these will be the way that computer poetry will not admit flummery. Lacking 'common sense', AI models often fulfil the incorrect tasks. So a robot trained to play football by touching the ball as many times as possible develops the strategy of standing next to the ball and vibrating rapidly. A programme designed to tell when cows are 'in oestrous' – a condition they're in once every twenty days – happily achieves a 95 percent accuracy by predicting every day that they weren't.

These cases are asinine, but serve to illustrate how machines are liable to give us what we *say* we want, rather than what we *actually* want. And ironically thereby they expose the imprecision in our understanding of our own desires. Exploring poetry in AI would help, in its process rather than its products, to clarify both what we actually consider poetry at all, but also what we consider meritorious in poetry. We'd learn not what we *say* we want from poems, but what we *actually* want. Whether computers succeed in providing that then becomes more or less beside the point.

Poetry, for me, is simply a means to an end. The end is in embracing existence in its fullness; to be nudged from habituation and numbness to it. It so happens that there is no other means, that I know of, to pursue this project nearly so fully. I think this is because poetry requires attention to language, that strange building; its signifier and its signified simultaneously. It requires intuition, empathy and musical sensibility to be attuned at the same time as our faculties of ratiocination. These facets of us – with the emotional hopelessly jumbled with the intellectual – are baked-in to the very form of the form. Further, poetry's strange expressive novelties require us to remain perpetually alert to the fact that reading and sense-making is a communal activity: it brings us back to our fundamental connectedness with networks beyond ourselves. But if the unthinkable richness of complexity that these features possess brings us to the world anew, it also motivates the colossal amount of total bullshit spoken about the artform.

This is key: it seems that computers' relentless literality gives us an opportunity to reject the bluster, the hyper-exclusive critical-theory academese, the mystic wiffle, the exculpatory buffalo, the vapid and vapidifying blurb-talk, the pseudo-religious gerrymander of spirit, the shabby flotilla of 'urgent new voices' and Derridean hauntology. It's an opportunity to actually – in a way which will allow us to express clearly and persuasively the merits of our artform, rather than preserving its social cache by implicitly insisting that most people are too dumb to get at it – figure out what poetry is, how it

works, what it gives us and what we like. The fact that the 'we' here will be highly mutable, and produce a huge variety of these answers, is both inevitable as well as the kind of unequivocal proof that we as a community would find valuable.

LLMs currently pose no challenge to humans in the composition of poetry, because of the amount of data they require for training. Nor does poets' work being used to train LLMs make a significant difference to the workings of such software. Nonetheless, as an area of thought, they offer significant opportunities for valuable reflection on the processes and unconscious patterns we bring to poetry by humans. With climate change's now unavoidable effects drawing nearer, there's a very severe cliff in the middle-near future over which our levels of energy production will drop. The server farms and closed-loop liquid-cooled data centres necessary for ChatGPT and Bard cannot outlive our incredible historical moment. I propose that we take this opportunity to experiment with poetry and AI while we still can.

# Ingarani / England

### Five poems, from Buxton, Rye, Lewes and Little Tew

#### GREGORY O'BRIEN

## Skulk

What if the distances
between towns
were measured
in foxes

as they are
in Charlbury,
a considerable skulk
from here

the woods also
measured in foxes,
hours calculated
in fox-hours,

elevation in
fox-height. The day's mischief
a rare sheepskin.
A hound population means

fewer foxes – an alternative
measure, the towns herded
closer together,
dogged, resistant,

and us, here
on our high mound,
earth of their earth,
dressed for the weather,

swallowed whole
in our bearish
jacketry, the perfect winter
of our pelts.

## Buxtonian

The tower minus the geese, the snow,
the birch trees

The birch trees minus the snow,
the geese, the tower

The geese minus the birch trees,
the tower, the snow

The snow minus the geese, the birch
trees, the tower.

# Little Tew (I)

Or was it just sky, this consistency?
  Look up. The crows

are *with us*. Max has been
studying the matter.

Nothing would fly
without them. This we know. A darkness

  around the edges of
most things, or at its centre. Blackest comedy

of the silhouetted bird-tree,
  from which the piano's

chattering apprentice
looks down upon hamlet,
    music room, us.

*The crows are on our side...*

Believe this – the bird
  in your ear. But not

as it was once
  in a tree.

# The South

This I was not opposed to:
Vanessa tarrying between
pond and water tower,

the garden a keyboard upon which played
fork and trowel.
Beyond her decorated windowsill,

the fields were nothing
if not attentive, studious almost
in their barrenness,

their occasion. Calm that follows
the storm, gull that follows the fishing boat,
broom that follows the leaf...

But what is it that follows
love? Another love? Step
softly. Consider the underfoot. I ask you.

# Little Tew (II)

The air made icebergs of us,
walking the garden path, worm-wet and clammy
yet somehow definitive. Small animals

like cameras followed, keeping
their distance, their mole-hill tripods
and measured gaze. Everything perfect

in its place, a silence rendered or
music to our ears. Above the glass roof
my lack of knowledge of birds

whirled and regrouped, leaving me none
the wiser. The encompassing woodlands I knew
only as well as they knew me.

The watching, waiting world consumed
by seasonal quiet: sans serif trees turning
back into trees, typewritten birds into birds.

# On Accidentally Finding a Handwritten Poem of Philip Larkin's in a Book by Lawrence Durrell

## PHILIP TERRY

When my father died suddenly and unexpectedly in 2004, he left behind an eclectic collection of books, accumulated over a lifetime, and twenty-four jars of marmalade, which my mother had made the day before. His assortment of Catalan books, which made the plank and brick bookshelf they were kept on sag precariously in the middle, and which contained over a thousand items – he was the founder of the Anglo-Catalan Association, and himself wrote books in Catalan – we donated to the Albert Sloman library at the University of Essex, where he had worked in the Department of Literature with Robert Lowell and John Barrell, after moving from Queen's University Belfast in the early 1970s. The other books we mostly gave away, or sold to second-hand bookshops, or distributed around the family. Most of the poetry I kept for myself, and have been reading my way through ever since. And it's probably no coincidence that it was shortly after this date that I started to *write* poetry, in a misguided attempt, I sometimes think, not to let go of my father. It was to be some years, eighteen to be precise, before I picked up his copy of Lawrence Durrell's poems *On Seeming To Presume* (1948) from my office one afternoon and took it home to read in the evening. On opening it, later the same day, I found some loose leaf papers inside the dust jacket: a review of the book by H.A.L. Craig clipped from the *Spectator* of 4 March 1949, two poems in my father's hand, 'Ingleborough' and 'Roland', one untitled poem in an unknown hand which reads 'The terrible minute / Which holds / A bullet or a poem / Folds in its void / The ambiguous faces / Of the dead', written alongside two versions of another untitled short poem, and a fifth poem entitled 'At First' and signed PAL (with three dots beneath the signature). The fifth poem was immediately recognisable as one of Philip Larkin's, published in *The Whitsun Weddings* under the slightly different title 'First Sight', and some rapid detective work at the Philip Larkin Archives at the University of Hull revealed that Larkin, early in his career, had indeed been in the habit of signing his name as PAL, Philip Arthur Larkin, characteristically with three dots beneath the autograph, one beneath each of the letters. My father, I guessed, must have lent the volume to Larkin, and it had been returned with this early draft of 'First Sight' as a thank you. I was excited. Here was a handwritten poem of Larkin's, which is a rare thing – in 2013 a handwritten version of 'Love' was sold by Bonhams for £7,500 – and although it was almost identical to the published poem, it had two slight but significant differences. One of these was the title, the other was a deletion in the first line of the second stanza where Larkin had changed 'yew' to 'ewe'. The poem, beginning 'Lambs that learn to walk in snow', describes how the lambs meet 'a vast unwelcome', find only 'a wretched width of cold'. The second stanza, in the handwritten version, looks like this:

As they wait beside the ewe,
Her fleeces wetly caked, there lies
Hidden round them, waiting too,
Earth's immeasurable surprise.
They could not grasp it if they knew,
What so soon will wake and grow
Utterly unlike the snow.

The change, slight as it is, gives us a tantalising glimpse of Larkin at work. His first thought, 'wait beside the yew', works perfectly well – we picture the lamb huddling beneath the overhanging branches of the evergreen in winter – were it not for the fact (something my father would have been quick to point out, and perhaps did) that yews, because they are poisonous to livestock, were grown mainly in churchyards, precisely to keep them away from farm animals. So 'yew' won't do, and Larkin's substitution of the homophone 'ewe' is at once simple and ingenious. And yet we lose something that was originally there in the second line, and that is the *likeness* of a yew's branches when covered in snow to fleeces – 'her fleeces wetly caked' (or, as the line most likely ran in an earlier draft, 'its fleeces...'). The line fits the ewe too, of course, but now in a literal and no longer a metaphoric way, though a reader might be forgiven for wondering why this particular ewe has more than one fleece, unless 'fleeces' here refers to the fleeces of her offspring that now surround her, and why Larkin didn't simply change this line to read 'Her fleece'. Whatever the truth of the matter, Larkin chose not to change this, and he had plenty of time to do so between writing the poem, in 1956, and publishing it, in 1964.

When I came across the Larkin poem tucked into the Durrell volume I sent it to a number of my poetry friends, pointing out the deletion. And I immediately decided I'd keep it rather than put it up for auction. The story might have ended there, but then I started wondering why Larkin had sent this particular poem to my father. In his essay 'Larkin in Belfast' my father writes about how they both joined the staff of Queen's University in October 1950, and quickly began going on walks along the Lagan and swapping books, and here he describes too their mutual admiration for one of the women librarians, Molly Sellar: 'both Philip and I had long admired her Scottish good sense and self-effacing cheerfulness, just as we appreciated her ability to produce late-night coffee and, on one occasion, porridge.' Without putting it in so many words, the essay also hints at a nascent rivalry for Molly's attention. My father describes, in particular, a double performance by Chris Barber and his Band early in 1955, on a Friday evening and a Saturday afternoon. With barely-repressed triumph, he writes: 'Philip had invited Molly to go with him on the Friday (though he didn't know it, we had agreed to get engaged the day before); my own turn came on the Saturday, when Philip, having hugely enjoyed the previous night's proceedings, decided to go a second time.' The notion of a hidden rivalry gains support from the fact that Larkin, a keen amateur photographer, had taken several photographs of Molly posing lithely in an elegant handknitted sweater, four of which appeared in the volume *The Importance of Elsewhere: Philip Larkin's Photographs* (2015), with the caption: 'One woman, still unidentified, posed for ten prints in his Belfast room, adopting postures and expressions remarkably similar to those of Monica and Patsy when they were photographed in the same spot.' And I remember, shortly after the book was published, meeting a prominent member of the Larkin Society in a hotel in Palermo where he was talking about the book, and mentioned the unidentified woman, who I knew at the time to be my mother. When I asked her, on arriving home, if I should identify her, she said she'd prefer to keep it a mystery, but meanwhile somebody must have recognised the photograph, for it appears with her name beneath it in James Booth's biography, *Philip Larkin: Life, Art and Love* which came out the same year. Another hint at this rivalry is there in one of Larkin's letters of 6 March 1954, where he writes: 'Must close now as I am going to the *Film Society* (alone) & after to Jill McIver's with *Arthur & Molly* & no doubt dozens of other bastards.' When the letter was first printed, in the *Selected Letters of Philip Larkin* (1992), my parents, particularly my father, were very upset to read this, and couldn't understand why Larkin had referred to them as 'bastards'. For a long time, I thought that my parents were silly to take it so personally, but now I see that there was an element of the personal in it, and that their mistake was perhaps to take it too *literally*: they weren't bastards, Larkin was just expressing his feeling of having been left out in the cold (alone), excluded from the cosy world of couples. And it is this, or so it seems to me now, that explains why Larkin sent *this* poem, 'At First', to my father (the 'you', another homophone of 'yew', to whom it is addressed): Larkin *is* the lamb, left out in 'a wretched width of cold'. When did he send it? If the biographers are right that it was written in 1956 – though it's just possible that this handwritten draft belongs to an earlier date – then it was sent from Hull, where Larkin moved in 1955, the same year as the Barber concerts, and which is the subject of the poem 'Here', which opens *The Whitsun Weddings*, and which is there characterised by 'solitude', 'loneliness' and 'removed lives'. And seen from this perspective, the metaphor that is removed – the ewe's 'fleeces' becoming literal as 'yew' changes to 'ewe' – is now restored, as the whole poem becomes a metaphor for a love that the writer has been shut off from, and it seems to say that, just as the lamb can never *know* the miracle of spring that lies round the corner, so the poet will never know love. And Larkin's later title for the poem, 'First Sight', would seem to reflect this contextual reading – 'First Sight' suggests, most obviously, 'love at first sight' (Molly's long admired 'Scottish good sense and self-effacing cheerfulness') but here the word 'love' is erased, just as the word 'yew' is erased in the handwritten draft.

In my father's essay on Larkin in Belfast he lists some of the authors that he and Larkin most admired,

including Henry Green, the early Auden and Hardy, but there is no mention of Lawrence Durrell. Nor is there any note from Larkin giving his opinion of Durrell in the returned volume – there is not even a thank-you note. There is much about Durrell's book that Larkin would not have appreciated, especially the epigraph, in the French of Georges Blin and taken from *Le Sens de l'absurde*, which describes the writer's task in an existentialist vein, coming to terms with the absurdity of existence. But there are other notes hit by Durrell that strike me as very Larkinesque, and that suggest that Larkin might well have taken to, and taken something from, the book. The line 'They pour the poison in' from the title poem 'On Seeming To Presume' (itself like a Larkin title) is reminiscent of 'This Be The Verse' (1971) with its 'They fill you with the faults they had'. Then there is the ending flourish of the poem 'In the Garden: Villa Cleobolus' where Durrell meditates on capturing the now in all its complexity in a poem:

Perhaps not this: but somehow, yes,
To outflank the personal neurasthenia
That lies beyond in each expiring kiss:
Bring joy, as lustrous on this dish
The painted dancers motionless in play
Spin for eternity, describing for us all
The natural history of the human wish.

What Durrell achieves here is what Borges, in his essay 'The Wall and the Books', calls the 'immanence of a revelation that does not take place', and which he defines as 'the aesthetic fact'. It echoes the end of Keats's 'Ode on a Grecian Urn', and it is precisely what characterises the mature Larkin, suggesting that he read very closely and internalised the book my father had sent him, even if he sent back a 'cold' poem. It is a trait which is visible not only in 'First Sight' itself, where the revelation that is spring is hidden from the lamb's understanding, but in many of the poems in *The Whitsun Weddings*, 'Here', 'Dockery and Son', 'An Arundel Tomb', and in the evanescent ending of 'The Whitsun Weddings' itself:

There we were aimed. And as we raced across
    Bright knots of rail
Past standing Pullmans, walls of blackened moss
Came close, and it was nearly done, this frail
Travelling coincidence; and what it held
Stood ready to be loosed with all the power
That being changed can give. We slowed again,
And as the tightened brakes took hold, there swelled
A sense of falling, like an arrow-shower
Sent out of sight, somewhere becoming rain.

The notion of an imminent revelation that refuses to materialise is something that has haunted this essay too, which has continued to proliferate more questions than answers. One of these is, why would my father have included his own poems in the volume if this was exchanged in 1956? In the essay on their time in Belfast, he says that he gave up writing poems shortly after seeing Larkin's. My father recounts how he mentioned a poem of his that had appeared in a local magazine in early 1951. 'Since its theme was photography,' he writes, 'a subject in which I knew Philip was interested, I showed it to him and, after what now seems an impossibly benevolent comment, he remarked quite casually that he himself had a privately printed collection of poems due out very shortly and that he would give me a copy when it appeared. This, of course, turned out to be *XX Poems*, now an immensely valuable collector's item, whose publishing history is well-known.' He goes on to say: 'One effect of *XX Poems* was to stop me writing poems myself'. And then it struck me that, since my father included his own poems inside the dust jacket of *On Seeming To Presume*, he must have lent Larkin the Durrell volume *before* the publication of *XX Poems*, that is before 1951. If that's right, and if Larkin returned it in 1956, the year he wrote 'First Sight', this means that Larkin had hung on to the volume for a very long time, something in the region of six years, which, if it had been a library book, would have incurred a hefty fine. If Larkin held on to the book for six years, it certainly helps explain how he came to know its poems so well.

But it also helps explain something else. Looking at Larkin's handwriting in 'At First' and comparing it with the poems in the unidentified handwriting, while the two hands are at first sight a little different, closer inspection does reveal some clear similarities: lower case 'd's' are truncated to resemble 'a's'; capital 'I's' look more like underlined lower case 't's' with a cross bar; lower case 'e's' and 'c's' are indistinguishable. The handwriting, in a word, is very similar, and if there are differences, these differences can easily be explained by the fact that the handwriting samples are separated by *six years*. And if, at first glance, the poems don't resemble what we now think of as a Larkin poem – they are either imperfectly rhymed or unrhymed, for one thing – their romantic world of introspection and dream comes straight out of the poems Larkin published in 1945 in *The North Ship*, which contains much that is aphoristic, too, in the manner of these handwritten drafts. Then, like the poems which Larkin published up to and including *XX Poems*, they are untitled. The second of the poems, in its second draft, though it still reads like a sketch, groping its way towards its rhymes, goes like this:

Locked
In the naked moment
The watcher holds his breath
For the unbidden rose
Which cleaves
The pavement of his dream

In many respects, this still belongs to the world of *The North Ship*: it has the aphoristic brevity of poem XXVI, and the dream of X, XI, XXI, XXII and XXV, while the 'watcher' (a word which, in *The North Ship*, is associated specifically with the watching poet) fits with this book's use of abstracted personae or types like the 'horseman' of XIV, the 'lovers' of XVI and the 'mourners' of XVII.

Other aspects of the poem, however, can be seen as a direct response to Durrell: Larkin's 'Locked / in the naked moment' picks up on lines in the penultimate stanza of Durrell's 'In the Garden: Villa Cleobolus' ('Within a poem locked'). And then the combination of watcher, waiting, and expecting something to appear calls to mind the world of the photographer, with which Larkin so strongly identified. And all of this combines to surprise me into thinking something which borders on the astonishing: in this one slim volume, published in 1948, and which for eighteen years lay unread in my office, there have lain concealed for almost seventy years, as in a poetic time capsule, what must be some of the last poems my father ever wrote; a handwritten and signed draft of a poem in Larkin's mature style, where we catch Larkin in the act of revising his work, and this in a way that sheds new light on the poem's evolution: evidence of a little-known poetic influence on Larkin; and perhaps the last, and previously unknown, handwritten drafts of poems in a style that Larkin was to definitively abandon with the publication of *The Less Deceived* in 1955.

# Four Poems

## ÉIREANN LORSUNG

## Waterway connecting the city to the sea: image and commentary

Contrary
to popular
opinion it
exists
for reasons
other than
to home
the weird
dog-faced
dolphins
left stranded
in fresh
water at
the end
of the late
middle ages.

*– to support the production
of flax, which must ret
in its flood plain; and to be home
to orchards of pomegranates,
which bristle on improbable
trees above it; and to host citrus,
and olive groves; to be the imagined
land on which anything is possible;
to lift a flight of birds out
of the picture in a V-
formation; to suffer the humid
bodies of female hermits;
and to reflect the sky;
and to subside into the ground;
and to return in the spring,
with the thaw, the very image of mercy.*

## Signification

Let *angel* mean *musician*. Momentarily.
Let *painter* mean *the figures on
flat ground*. Let *Adam* mean the *tuft* in *tufted
vetch*. Let *borage* stand for *city on*

a hill. Let *Hubert* bear the letter *younger
bro*. Let *personage* bring *ma-
sterpiece* to bear. *Geography* the *on-
of onlooker*. Let *earth* take on

the meaning *sacrifice*. Let *Gentiles* signify
*The Mystic Lamb. Inspiration*
mean only *breath comes in*. Let *testimony*
mean that *I was There*. Let *hand* mean *enter*

*side*, and *man*, and *doubt. Color* only *light*.
Let *painting*, in the end, mean just *Amen*.

## Postcard to Shana with image of blackbirds

It took me *this long* to realize that when the poet
said blackbirds, he meant *blackbirds*: pointing

to the world. (That's just an image in a poem,
though.) Outside, in our now of April rain, two

blackbirds are pulling worms through the lawn's
thatch. It's spring, and soon no one will have

to resemble anyone except their younger self,
who ran out of university buildings in rain

like this, the fine rain of early spring, to steal
daffodils from the sleeping grounds. Come, write

back to me: my feet are soaking in the sodden grass.
My hands are raw from cold and wet. The table's

set. The light goes through green glass. A jar
of flowers. Rain through grapevine on the panes.

Every warm thing from our girlhood calls us now.
Blackbirds. Poems. The world: its tablecloths

and rainy mornings, cities, hands, and flowers.
Its universities. Its sense of always coming to an end.

## Postcard to Shana with photograph of
## Floraliën Ghent, 1913

Everyone I know is losing something this year. Yesterday
I heard the cuckoo for the first time, which means

it's really spring. Since I last wrote, invisible teams of gardeners
went to work all over Ghent, only their secateurs catching

light; in days the entire city was transformed.
Gardenias, azaleas. A young man stood near a shallow

pool breaking flowers from a peach branch, setting
them in water. Everything unrecognizable in its new

botanical clothes. You know I have been working
in an orchard of my own: peach tree and cherry

trees; apples; plum. The lawn is broken bright with daffodils.
I thought, *if I leave him I will lose the garden*

*I made.* I know I can make another garden anytime.
Nevertheless (oh – the lambs are playing now, again!), I stayed.

# Anthony Hecht in Kindless Dark

## TONY ROBERTS

Anthony Hecht (1923–2004) was the Prospero of his generation of American poets: magical, manipulative and melancholic. His poems could be extravagantly ornate or plain-speaking, impersonal and personal by turns, with perspectives changing even within poems in order to create unconventional discontinuities. The poet's self is fragmented into countless, generally suffering, personae.

In the past twenty-five years, interest in Hecht's work has hardly flagged. He is in fine form in a 1999 book-length interview, *Anthony Hecht in conversation with Philip Hoy* (one of those excellent 'Between the Lines' publications) and in the *Selected Letters*, edited by Jonathan F.S. Post in 2013. Last year saw the publication of both *Late Romance: Anthony Hecht – A Poet's Life* by David Yezzi and the *Collected Poems of Anthony Hecht: including late and uncollected work*, again edited by Hoy.

While anchored to a modern sensibility, Hecht's poetry ranges through the centuries to explore instances of cruelty and suffering which illustrate the human condition. He is most memorable on the dark side of experience. He takes his text from Job 5:7:

The river worms through the snow plain
In kindless darks.
And man is born to sorrow and to pain
As surely as the sparks
Fly upward.

In 'The Venetian Vespers' a troubled American in a decaying Venice acknowledges 'those first precocious hints of hell, / Those intuitions of living desolation / That last a lifetime'. Scenes of horror abound in the poems. Yet Hecht also has other moods and preoccupations. He can render in an exact way how the senses respond to fleeting scenes ('The air is a smear of ashes / With a cool taste of coins'; 'The gentle graphite veil / Of rain that makes of the world a steel engraving'). He can be playful and witty, as in 'The Dover Bitch', his Haydn-Shakespeare masque 'A Love for Four Voices', or in 'A Lot of Night Music', where he takes a satirical swipe at fellow poets:

They speak in tongues, no doubt;
High glossolalia, runic gibberish.
Some are like desert saints,
Wheat-germ ascetics, draped in pelt and clout.
Some come in schools, like fish.

Both the collected poems and the biography illustrate the numerous influences on this consummate formalist's poetry. In his early career Eliot figured significantly, though others were heard and quoted: the Bible, the classical poets and, in particular, Shakespeare. The list continues from Herbert to his own time and includes Auden, whom he knew and wrote on, and Brodsky, a close friend he translated. In *True Friendship* (2010) Christopher Ricks noted, 'For a poet with Hecht's disposition toward old poems in the creation of new poems, literary allusion is at once inevitable, inviolable, and eager not to violate.' And Hecht is everywhere allusive. As he explained in a 1988 interview: 'As I am writing, certain texts that have meant much to me by their power or beauty are summoned by the theme or thoughts that preoccupy me, and when this happens I sometimes try to work a relevant phrase or passage into the fabric of my own poem as seamlessly as possible, so that the knowing reader will spot it, but another reader will not be intimidated by obscure illusions.'

Given the many allusions to literature, art and music, the fifty pages of textual notes in the handsome, six-hundred-page *Collected Poems* (by Philip Hoy and the late J.D. McClatchy) are welcome. To take one example: the twelve-verse poem 'The Cost' has ten explanatory notes relating to contemporary and ancient Rome, mythology, *Othello* and *Hamlet*, Calder the mobile artist, St. Gregory, Yeats and, overshadowing all, the Vietnam War. Book titles (*Millions of Strange Shadows*), poem titles ('Alceste in the Wilderness'), epigraphs (*'But to the girdle do the gods inherit / Beneath is all the fiend's'*), as well as phrases in poems, often borrow from others.

Hecht's command of detail is particularly impressive when painting 'water's anamorphosis', clouds and rain, early mornings and window scenes. What he depicts is the effect of light and shadow on these phenomena. They provide for him the challenge a painter faces in depicting nature and offer the chance for bravura display:

> The seamed, impastoed bark,
> The cool, imperial certainty of stone,
> Antique leaf-lace, all these are bathed in a dark
> Mushroom and mineral odor of their own
> ('The Lull')

Precision of expression is central to Hecht's purpose. 'To give one's whole attention to such a sight / Is a sort of blessedness', he writes in one poem. 'One of the things I learned from Bishop, from Hardy, from Frost,' he told Hoy, 'concerned particularity and clarity of seeing. Seen with enough precision, things become wonderful.'

In *Late Romance* David Yezzi offers a context for the paradoxes and preoccupations of a life lived with much less certainty than the poems. He has a gruelling story to tell and tells it with pace, while establishing a personality frequently on the verge of unravelling. Hecht once said he feared insanity, which is unsurprising given a deeply unhappy childhood, his hard wartime experiences, a difficult marriage and painful divorce, and subsequent breakdowns:

> This is your nightmare. Those cold hands are yours.
> The pain in the drunken singing is your pain.
> Morning will taste of bitterness again.
> The heart turns to a stone, but it endures.
> ('Clair de Lune')

Born into a dysfunctional but affluent New York Jewish family, Hecht endured the early indifference of his parents: a weak-willed, unstable father who repeatedly failed in business and a dominant mother who lavished her attentions on a handicapped brother, Roger, later also a poet and something of a lifelong shadow to his older brother. Hecht was frequently anxious and depressed, an outsider who slowly found some acceptance through his acting and in poetry while studying at Bard College, where he later taught.

During the Second World War, after an army translation programme for which he had enlisted was shut down, he joined the 97th Infantry Division in Europe. He decided he would not fire his weapon against the enemy in combat. Later he regretted his failure to support his fellow soldiers. Eventually he was assigned to interviewing French survivors in the Flossenbürg concentration camp, which further damaged him. War anecdotes and images recur in his work, in such poems as 'Sacrifice', 'The Venetian Vespers' and 'The Hunt'. As Yezzi says, 'His most accomplished war poems deal with the moral compromise and helplessness associated with combat and the Holocaust. But even when he's not writing explicitly about the war, trauma inheres in the imagery.' 'Still Life', for instance, offers as a dawn scene a sensitively evoked nightmare:

> As in a water-surface I behold
>     The first, soft, peach decree
> Of light, its pale, inaudible commands.
> I stand beneath a pine-tree in the cold,
> Just before dawn, somewhere in Germany,
> A cold, wet, Garand rifle in my hands.

In light of these experiences, it is no surprise that the darkened tone of Hecht's intellect overwhelmed his subjects from the start. The appropriately named *The Hard Hours*, his 1968 Pulitzer Prize collection, begins with 'A Hill', with 'the plain bitterness' of a hallucination of childhood physical constraint. The collection draws us into a powerfully disturbing, deeply unsettled and vengeful world, where an awesome-winged predator disturbs two lovers; the Emperor Valerian is flayed alive; we witness the Dance of Death, the Seven Deadly Sins, the Tower of London and an old woman's suffering a vision of the devil. There are concentration camps; an eyeless corpse; graves and PTSD victims. Darkness and the dead deny the little wry humour in the book. Yet the poet later worried that in some of the poems his art had distanced reality too much.

The war caused Hecht to finally affirm his Jewishness. From then on, the fate of 'the burning, voiceless Jews' haunted him. In poem after poem they are gone, 'as if all history were deciduous'. 'Samson' remembers the murder of the little boys in the shul at Lodz, while in 'The Book of Yolek' it is the murdered child of a murdered Warsaw orphanage ('Though they killed him in the camp they sent him to, / He will walk in as you're sitting down to a meal.') 'Death the Whore' ends, 'As for the winter scene of which I spoke – The smoke, my dear, the smoke. I am the smoke.' And the renowned 'More Light! More Light!' (said to have been

Goethe's last words) begins with the torture of a Renaissance martyr before switching to an act of evil in a German wood at Buchenwald: 'Nor light from the shrine at Weimar beyond the hill / Nor light from heaven appeared.'

After reconciliation with his parents, Hecht spent time at Kenyon College on the G.I. Bill, where he placed poems in *The Kenyon Review*. He made use of his pain, not in a confessional manner, but as Yezzi suggests 'more in keeping with his New Critical sensibilities', since he had become a protégé of both his teacher John Crowe Ransom and Alan Tate: 'Instead of personal disclosure he preferred what Eliot called the third voice of poetry, the dramatic voice, which nevertheless closely shadows the personal.' We read into the poet's life in such poems as 'Apprehensions', 'Circles' and 'Aubade'.

In 1951 Hecht began his love affair with Italy under the auspices of a first American Academy of Arts and Letters fellowship. He married three years later and subsequently taught at Smith and then the University of Rochester from 1967. A second, happy marriage took place in 1971 when, in his late forties, he met a former student, Helen D'Alessandro – hence the biography's title. Until then Hecht seems to have ground out a life, despite enjoying continuing success (eventually including the Bollingen Prize and the National Medal of Arts). His later career involved other collections of poems, visiting professorships at Harvard and Yale and a move to Georgetown University, from where he retired.

Although by some accounts a difficult man and demanding teacher – one who assumed the mantle of poet with gravity – Hecht nevertheless had a strong sociable streak. He could be popular company, being witty, handsome and stylish. He regularly dedicated poems to friends and became a frequent elegist. Yezzi's problem in the biography is to balance his frequent psychologising of the inner man with the robust public figure. Two-thirds into the book he reminds the reader that, 'It's not that Hecht had been morose this whole time; his affect was more stoic than lugubrious. But there was an underlying angst; he had come to doubt his own worth.'

For all its cultured craftmanship, one wonders how Hecht's poetry will be remembered in the future. Perhaps it is as the poet 'able to horrify' (in William Logan's phrase) that he best speaks to *our* war-torn times, as a dramatic poet who brings, like Ariel, the warning cry, 'Hell is empty and all the devils are here'.

# Nothingness

### STANLEY MOSS

When I see a video of someone named
Stanley David Moss, I ask,
'Is this a snapshot of anyone I know?'
If God is, He knows exactly who He is.
I am, but I don't know who I am.
When you get older, your face's skin,
the skin around your body changes,
shrinks, but not your nose and ears.

What is it like to be 98?
When I read the small type of *The New York Times*,
I can't help reading two lines at the same time.
After reading a page, you disrespect the writer
for no reason but your eyes.
I keep my word, but I'm not someone
who keeps looking like himself.

I refuse to guess who I am.
On my laptop, I'm not Stanley David Moss.
I look a little like my mother after she died.

Useful when you're 98, here's a metaphor.
I see some mourners following a body
wrapped in a shawl in a loved wooden box.
A surprise: they throw the coffin overboard
into a river. My coffin crashes into rocks, opens.
A sunfish thinks my wrinkles are worms. He bites me.
Again and again, I ask God
to tell me who He is.
I am this metaphor,
I am a camera without film
that takes photos of who I am.

# On First Looking into Dylan Thomas – II

## ANDREW McNEILLIE

As was worldwide headline news at the time, Dylan Thomas died tragically, on 9 November 1953, at the Chelsea Hotel, in Greenwich Village, NYC. He was thirty-nine. A serious excess of alcohol was involved but there were other critical factors obscured in the case. And so, prematurely, as W.H. Auden said on the occasion of Yeats's death, Dylan Thomas 'became his admirers'. But not only them. He also became his detractors, never in short supply, especially among the university-educated English post-war literati; and the victim too of mythologisers and sensationalists, ardent to present him as a hard-drinking *enfant terrible*, an inspired Welsh 'genius' who knew not what he did. That is, much as was done for Brendan Behan, who has only recently begun to be properly rehabilitated. What's more, in Thomas's case, he died just when on the cusp of financial success, the prospect of a collaboration with Igor Stravinsky being firmly established (they met in New York to discuss it), and an end to his terrible money worries in sight. How many 'British' literary contemporaries of Thomas ever had such a prospect?

It has to be said that, like Behan, Thomas, who in his youth styled himself as the Rimbaud of Cwmdonkin Drive (without, it is said, ever having read Rimbaud)[1], had played more than a little into the hands of the sensation mongers and romantics. He was delinquent, both as a schoolboy and occasionally as a man (not least in failing to file tax returns: a Faustian forfeit that did much to turn the screw on his final undoing, luring him to America for the money), and he was a performer. He played the heavy drinker. But there are many to bear witness that, generally, he took his preferred poison (beer) in quite modest doses. He was no alcoholic like Behan, or, as became the fate, among his friends and great admirers, of Louis MacNeice; and, tragically in the next generation, Derek Mahon, whose short essay on Thomas is one of the best and most judicious ever written about him.[2]

Thomas participated much on leaving school in Swansea amateur dramatics. He could carry a part so well (including once surviving being miscast as Oliver Cromwell), he might have had a career as an actor. And in one respect he did, in the broadcasting studio, to which his characteristically sonorous version of Received English and a remarkable gift for mimicry were ideally suited. He was a very funny man, skilled in self-mockery. When he read his poems, he affected the bardic role. It was a Welsh thing, influenced by the pulpit oratory of the chapel, and coloured by that sing-song cadence expressed in Welsh as *hwyl*. Grand and 'bardic' it was, though Thomas's voice carried scant trace of Welsh inflection – 'speaks rather fancy' was the way he put it in his 1947 broadcast 'Return Journey', as did his Welsh-speaking, intensely irascible, schoolmaster father.

The bardic approach to reading aloud also said that poetry is not prose and demands to be differentiated by heightened or otherwise distinctive delivery. Yeats and Eliot, in a tradition that goes back, on aural record, to Tennyson, similarly affected a special poetic voice when they intoned rather than read their poems aloud. So did Wallace Stevens. That style has now largely passed in the English language tradition. Ted Hughes went in for it somewhat. Geoffrey Hill, who, though English-born, had Welsh blood in him, about which he romanced considerably, and whose earliest poems were directly influenced by Thomas, was the most notable recent exponent of a heightened reading style (even rivalling Thomas's recording of G.M. Hopkins's most challenging 'The Leaden Echo and the Golden Echo' with one of his own). Of Thomas's reading voice, Hill once said to me, 'But *what* a way to do it!' when I suggested that sometimes the style embarrassed the poem.

It was a method which the poet-critic William Empson hoped no one after Thomas would ever try again. Not that Empson didn't admire Thomas's poetry. Not that he didn't like the man. He liked him enough to invite him to his wedding. But, more pertinently, during his ordeal as a peripatetic professor in war-torn China (1937–39), he chose to carry with him a book of Thomas's poems, because they provided 'inexhaustible' reading.[3]

That quality of inexhaustibility derives much from Thomas's conscientious craftsmanship, even where apparently random and, in terms of common-or-garden semantics, often barely intelligible effects prevail. Turn to 'I, in my intricate image' for a marvellous example of inexhaustible unintelligibility. It's quite a long poem and one Thomas thought unsatisfactory but still held on to. That wasn't at all unusual in his attitude to his poems. There they stand 'with all their crudities, doubts, and confusions', as he put it.[4] He does not decline to collect and publish them. Throw what you like at them, he seems to be saying. There they are, to test your bafflement, or impatience. Such a work as 'Altarwise by Owl-light', for example, with its 'gentleman of wounds',

---

1 But can that be true and who can be so sure? He might have read 'Le Bateau ivre' in translation, for example. That would have been up his street, in both subject matter, energy, and method.

2 Derek Mahon, 'Prospects of the Sea,' *Selected Prose* (Gallery Books, 2012).

3 John Haffenden, *William Empson: Among the Mandarins* (OUP, 2005), p. 314.

4 In his 'Note' to the *Collected Poems* (1952). 'I, in my intricate image' was the opening poem in Thomas's second collection, *Twenty-five Poems* (1936), *Collected Poems*, pp. 35-8.

its Rip van Winkle, 'two-gunned Gabriel', 'Jonah's Moby' and 'Jack Christ' not only rewards patience and dwelling, it delivers immediate, destabilising shocks that surely you don't have to be sixteen to appreciate. The same can be said of many of them. Or have your arteries hardened before their time? Of course Thomas's concealed connections or transitions challenge logic, but what poetry is written for logicians? They have their own modes of conduct 'whereof one cannot speak, thereof one must be silent'. How verbally and rhetorically impoverished much poetry has become since Thomas's heyday. Except perhaps in the work of Paul Muldoon, who also has a distinctly mannered approach to reading aloud.

The 'Intricate image' poem was written during an extended, solitary stay in a remote corner of Co. Donegal, at Meenacross, near Glencolumkille. It alludes in passing to the 'stony lockers' of Aran, suggesting perhaps that while in the country, Thomas had seen Robert Flaherty's movie *Man of Aran* (1934), though there is no other evidence to show he did, or that he ever visited the Aran Islands. (The painter Augustus John once did, but not in Thomas's company.) Such was the way Thomas drew together seemingly random elements, perhaps in this case from a newspaper article. It was during that time in the summer of 1935, call it a time in the wilderness, that Thomas, he was still not yet twenty-one, discovered how profoundly he disliked the outdoors. How he craved, while there, the inner world of literary and musical invention and experiment that he had enjoyed in suburban Swansea in the company of his friends. Above all such friends was the composer Daniel Jones (see the story 'The Fight'), to whom Thomas told all, in a long *tour-de-force* of a letter. Jones said that after Donegal, Thomas came back a changed man, with an altered focus and different sense of purpose. Though this might also have been determined to a degree by his growing reputation as a poet, as it drew him towards fame.

Thomas was from the start a maker and constructor of poems, in the humble spirit of an older tradition. But his poetics weren't traditional, though his themes frequently were. They were of his own making and largely without clear precedent. That's what makes the poems so startling and, in a positive sense, alienating. They haul you up before your expectations, rather as *Finnegans Wake* can do. As with the *Wake*, moments of lucidity surface from the ambient word noise (and deeply-buried allusions) all the more forcefully when they do. It's startling too that the majority of Thomas's poems were written or else begun in draft form by the time he was nineteen or twenty. The early ones have no titles but their first lines. They seem to be still arriving, discovering themselves, rather than serving a declared subject or idea. Rhythmic verbal expressions of 'a spiritual necessity or urge',[5] the poems find their way before our eyes (and ears), often to a resounding conclusion. They are never conventional. Thomas could talk about them with amusing detachment:

To choose what I should read tonight, I looked through seventy odd poems of mine, and found that many *are* odd indeed and that some may be poems. And I decided not to choose those that strike me, still, as pretty peculiar, but to stick to a few of the ones that do move a little way towards the state and destination I imagine I intended to be theirs when, in small rooms in Wales, arrogantly and devotedly I began them.[6]

For Thomas the idea of 'literature' came with a health warning. So too did academic study and criticism. He was fiercely independent and largely unperturbed by what others chose to say about his work. He knew his difference and his gift. No one was tougher-minded in pursuit of his craft or art. He certainly didn't see himself as any kind of visionary or prophet. Insofar as he was religious, it was as a celebrant before the wonder of creation. He rejoiced metaphysically in what we must call Nature (as we've seen he didn't like too much direct exposure to it; he was no nature poet) and he celebrated common humanity (and the *comédie humaine* – 'the common wild intelligence of the town')[7], notably in his later stories, and the play for voices *Under Milk Wood*. But he was no sociologist. He celebrated language, the human spirit, and the humane. His starting point, like that of the Scottish poet W.S. Graham, was that poems are made of words. Words are made of sounds. Poetry must be sounded and heard to be.

As he put it in his note to the *Collected Poems* of 1952, Thomas wrote 'for the love of Man and in praise of God'. These are surely rare motivations in the twentieth century. Thomas is remarkable in that he speaks from somewhere apart, in many ways from old biblical Wales, as lived in by his grandparents. (The poet's middle name 'Marlais' nods at this heritage, in the direction of a bardic great uncle.) It was his cultural (and ultimately geographical) apartness that made him the writer he was, that and his rapport with 'honest poverty', his courage to address the big themes of birth and death. He is something other, but not other-worldly. He wasn't a 'druid' of Ann Jones's broken body, so much as her 'bard on a raised hearth'.[8] There was nothing druidic about him.

---

5 See the opening to the otherwise satirical 'How to be a Poet, or The Ascent of Parnassus made Easy. A Worldly Lecture in two parts...', *Circus. The Pocket Review of our Time*, 1 April and 2 May 1950.

6 'On Reading One's Own Poems', *Quite Early One Morning* (1954), broadcast 24 September 1949.

7 See 'One Warm Saturday'.

8 See 'After the Funeral (In memory of Ann Jones)', first collected in *The Map of Love* (1939), *Collected Poems* (1952), p. 87. The phrase 'Druid of the Broken Body' was used by Aneirin Talfan Davies as a subtitle to his book *Dylan* (1964) 'An Assessment of Dylan Thomas as a Religious Poet'.

## A Thicket of Goldcrests

Sam Adams, *Letters from Wales: Memories and Encounters in Literature and Life* (Parthian) £20

Reviewed by Gwyneth Lewis

When I heard that Parthian was publishing a compendium of poet Sam Adams's 'Letters from Wales', I was overjoyed. *PN Review* has published one hundred and fifty-eight of Adams's letters since the 1990s, forming a body of cahiers of 'affective response' to the history and writing of Wales. Published alongside epistles from all corners of the world (I remember writing one from New York, about events marking the tenth anniversary of W.H. Auden's death), Adams's missives read together are a treasure trove of deep knowledge about Welsh culture. This is a tradition which the English think they know but don't and which, as Michael Schmidt notes in his introduction, resists both Anglo-Saxon integration and insularity. There's a good deal to be learned elsewhere from the particular conjunctions of Welsh politics and history: the first being that deep strands of English literature are inextricably formed by, through and with it.

Welsh writers have cause to be grateful to Sam Adams for his sustained and careful attention to Welsh writing. Adams is self-effacing and never mentions his own work as a poet – restraint that sometimes I wish others would observe. His prose is poetic in the best sense: he mentions the 'St Vitus's dance of TV in the corner' and, in Rhys Davies's flat, notices 'a small bronze of a naked youth, in the antique manner, with a full wineskin on his back, in the act of pouring wine into a beaker, his

image of the burden of self-expression in writing, joyfully borne', an exquisitely poised description of the creative life. In various essays, Adams evokes R.S. Thomas in a thicket of goldcrests. He layers memories of the Aust ferry across the Severn with an account of St Augustine insulting the Celtic bishops at their momentous meeting at that place, which led to the split between the Roman and the Celtic church (not that the Celts were touchy!).

Poets have always written psychogeography and Adams excels at this genre in both his prose and poetry. He's a great explorer of corners of Wales with literary associations, an attender of events and lectures. I was delighted to read an anecdote about him going astray somewhere outside Merthyr on the A470 and following a road sign to Twynyrodyn because he remembered a poem 'Ponies at Twynyrodyn' by his friend Meic Stephens. Such indirections seem to me entirely logical for a poet, and they get you to places that are not, strictly speaking, on the map. In a similar vein, Adams visits the border church of Clodock, where the great Raymond Williams is buried. He seeks out tiny parish churches such as Llanilltud Fawr in Llanrhaeadr-yng-Nghinmeirch (quite a mouthful) near Denbigh to see a stained-glass window of a Jesse Tree that was saved in the Reformation by being hidden in a buried chest by parishioners. These are the threads that tie a nation's history with its imagination of the future.

Adams's touchstone is the society of Gilfach Goch, the South Wales mining town in which he was born, and where Richard Llewellyn's *How Green Was My Valley* was allegedly set. Adams relays some delicious gossip about Llewellyn as a chancer, as a visiting writer to Aberystwyth University, and about his leaving bad debts and scandal in his wake in Patagonia. He notes that 'My sense of personal history, of rootedness, has become more demanding as I grow older', and he writes delightfully about the history of the area. Adams became a teacher and has made an important contribution to the promotion of Anglo-Welsh letters, not only as a poet but also as an editor and writer. He is a collector of antiquarian books and writes movingly about spending the compensation money for his father's industrial injury on a Golden Cockerel Press edition of the *Mabinogion*.

Jonathan Edwards, the editor of this collection, makes an excellent choice by opening the volume with 'My Grandfather's Lamp', from March 2020, which describes Adams cleaning his grandfather's mining lamp, the piece serves as a keynote for the whole collection. Having immersed the lamp in a new liquid,

> I found at its base a layer of the finest coal dust somehow displaced from recesses in the interior of the lamp. There it was; the very same black death that silted the lungs of my grandfather and snatched him away from us so shockingly in middle age, no more than a week after I was born. That is why I bear his name: Samuel.

I have a similar copy of a tiny Book of Psalms that my miner grandfather used to take underground. Its pages are impregnated with the same dust.

Adams is part of that generation of writers who, from the mid-twentieth century onwards, promoted the English-language literature of Wales in the so-called 'Second Flowering' that stemmed from magazines such as the *Anglo-Welsh Review*, founded by Keidrych Rhys. Poet and long-time editor of the magazine, Roland Mathias invited Adams to write for it, thus contributing to 'the enlargement of knowledge about writers and writing from Wales'. Scandalously, its descendent, the *New Anglo-Welsh Review,* along with *Planet Magazine: The Welsh Internationalist*, have both just lost their funding from the Books Council of Wales, an act of short-sighted vandalism. The demise of the Welsh Academi (a body separate from the Literature Wales / Llenyddiaeth Cymru promotion agency) is another sign of retreat from the progress that this important cohort of writers brought about.

Adams rightly praises the achievements of the writers of this 'Second Flowering' – whom he lists as Dylan Thomas, John Ormond, Leslie Norris, John Tripp, Dannie Abse, Vernon Watkins, Raymond Garlick, Meic Stephens and Harri Webb. The absence of women writers in this period is striking. I would have liked to hear more about those, such as Belinda Humfrey, Brenda Chamberlain, Lynette Roberts, Margiad Evans, Dorothy Williams, Christine Evans, Sally Roberts Jones, the half-Welsh Denise Levertov and many others. This was a generational blindness and by no means confined to Wales. Adams writes perceptively and often about contemporary female writers.

Adams is also eloquent about the changing of the guard, and he narrates a painful incident at a celebration to mark the fortieth anniversary of *Poetry Wales*. Robert Minhinnick opened the magazine to international writing and, for the occasion, edited an anthology but didn't include a poem by the magazine's founder, Meic Stephens, who remonstrated with him publicly. One of the best letters is a fully-deserved tribute to the work of Cary Archard who, when he was editor of *Poetry Wales*, began publishing pamphlets and books which developed into Seren and has given Welsh poetry national and international prominence. Reading *Poetry Wales*, Adams notes that, at one time, he would have known all the writers in the magazine personally, and that this is no longer the case. This is, perhaps, an inevitable – and healthy – change of emphasis between generations.

There is an inherent contradiction in a book of letters written for one audience – these were letters from Wales to the readers of the *PN Review* – being reprinted by a Welsh press for an internal audience in Wales. Letters from Wales become letters to Wales. This may not matter, because time acts like distance and it is important that we don't lose this recent literary history. *Letters from Wales*, with its generous appreciation of present achievements acts like a telescope, allowing us to view the deep landscape in which current work belongs.

Jonathan Edwards has excluded only five letters, and divided the remaining ones up into sections: 'On Writers', 'On Wales' and 'On the Literary Scene'. The distinctions seem rather arbitrary to me. Edwards has also chosen to run these groups in reverse chronological order, giving us a sense of delving back into the deep background to the present. There's a lot of repetition, which made me wish that he had excerpted more passages. This is the difference between writing for a magazine audience, which reads sporadically, and collating a book. For example, Adams is an expert on the work of T.J. Llewelyn Prichard, who wrote the tale of Twm Shôn Catti, the Welsh Robin Hood and who, we hear several times, lost his nose. Being obsessive, I read the book from start to finish, but many readers will want to dip in. The absence of an index, therefore, makes this less useful as a gazetteer of Welsh letters than it might have been.

Adams's letters have made me see afresh the things that I do know about the Welsh tradition, and has shown me the gaps in my knowledge. I came away from this volume with a long list of books that I haven't read. These include Edward Pugh's *Cambria Depicta* (Pugh was known as 'Professor of Miniature Painting'), Howel Harris's diary of his Methodist mission, Meic Stephens's *Rhys Davies: A Writer's Life,* Tony Conran's verse autobiography *What Brings You Here So Late?,* and Arthur Machen's memoir *Things Near and Far.* I didn't know anything about the work of T.H. Jones, who emigrated to Australia and whose biography by P. Bernard Jones and Don Dale-Jones I'm going to seek out. I also have a list of obscure churches up one-track lanes to venture down. We are very lucky to have, in Sam Adams, a sensitive, careful cultivator of Welsh poetry, and this collection is a treasure.

# A Philosophy of Time

Anne Carson, *Wrong Norma* (Vintage) £14.99

Reviewed by Valerie Duff-Strautmann

Anne Carson has made a career out of writing books made up of fragments, wildly-roped-together characters and pieces that defy genre. Her latest offering, *Wrong Norma*, feels very much part of her overall work, with a diverse cast of characters, a strange montage of typed lines interspersed as art throughout the text, together with an illustrated storyline about Paul Celan's visit to Martin Heideigger to Todtnauberg, ending simply, fatefully: 'Celan loaded his cart and started back down'. Carson herself says about *Wrong Norma* that it is 'a collection of writings about different things, like Joseph Conrad, Guantanamo, Flaubert, snow, poverty, Roget's Thesaurus, my Dad, Saturday night. The pieces are not linked. That's why I've called them "wrong"' – but the only 'wrongness' a seasoned Carson reader can find is her insistence on further fragmentation of genre – not poems, not stories, not plays, not visual art – pieces shaken together in an already fractured whirl of text.

As in previous work, the reader is set loose in the candy store of Carson's ruminations, finding well-known figures or those who appear only in Carson's mind – her friend Chandler, visitors from Iceland, Carson herself. In these selections, there are moments of grounded narrative (as in good film) or (again, as in good film) moments of being whisked along on the ride. Carson mentions the French director Eric Rohmer at various points ('do you like the films of Eric Rohmer'), and while there is a mixed bag of response (from 'no' to 'I find realistic techniques delightful'), the writing itself feels much more Fellini-esque, as real and imagined worlds blend and parade through each – for lack of a better word – station.

Beyond a flurry of form and characters, two ideas unify *Norma* – swimming and time. In '1=1', her friend Chandler has done his last drawing of the day: a fox ('red chalk in hand, it will be a fox, he likes a fox at the end of the day'). The 'she' who began her morning swimming sees this:

The finished fox drawing is under a streetlamp. It glows. He has used some sort of phosphorescent chalk and the fox, swimming in a blue-green jellylike lucidity of its own, is escaping all possible explanations. She stares at the blue-green. It has clearness, wetness, coolness, the deep-lit self-immersedness of water. *You made a lake*, she says, turning to him, but he is gone, now that it's night, off to wherever he goes when he is once again absolved. She stands awhile watching the fox swim, looking back on the day, pouring in and out. To be alive is just this pouring in and out. Ethics minimal. Try to swim without thinking how it looks. Beware mockery, mockery is too easy. She feels a breeze on her forehead, a night wind. The fox is stroking splashlessly forward. The fox does not fail.

The fox = the created thing, outside of time. What is compelling here seems to connect to a later moment, a search for the right words, in Carson's musings within the poem 'THRET: Part III: SWIMMING IN HÖLDER-LIN':

What I mean by accuracy is hard to sum up. There is a sentence of Hölderlin's that fell out of a book of fragments of his that I read once and then I couldn't find the book again. A sentence using the verb 'to swim' in the passive voice, as in:

*Mein Herz ist schwimmt in Zeit.*
My heart is swimmed in time.

This sentence seems to me an example of accuracy.

*Norma*, wrong in terms of cohesive progression, contains both knowledge and a logic of association. Carson's lines/sentences/insights appeal rationally and irrationally, with poetic accuracy. The swimming fox does not fail.

*Wrong Norma* takes a distanced look at our experience of time (and its accompanying grief), a writerly look at the grief of living. Carson's interest feels authentic, her exploration reflective and open. Considering the actions of a crow with its dead mate, she writes:

Do we understand how we ourselves grieve? Not really. Grief is big, grief is little, grief is cranky and comes at the wrong time, usually disguised as something

else. Chemically, a conspiracy of hormones, opioids and dopamine in the forebrain. I have a sense most grief is also deeply and horribly humorous but we're not supposed to say so. Aspirin for travellers, grief.

Is this where 'wrong' Norma applies? In Carson's receptiveness not only to blurred forms but blurred expectations, a willingness to take what comes and respond with multiple 'answers' – or none at all? Aspirin for travellers, we load our carts and start back down. The fox stroking splashlessly forward.

# Epistemic Job Spec

Jonathan Kramnick, *Criticism and Truth: Method in Literary Studies* (University of Chicago Press) $12.50

Reviewed by Mike Freeman

It may work in practice, but – as in the old joke – will it work in theory? And does it need re-branding if it's to compete in the academic market place? Earlier Jonathan Kramnick has written extensively about the porous membrane between the humanities and the sciences, but here the tenured professor assumes a collegiate benevolence, helping younger and would-be academics during the freeze on hiring and funding since the 2008 financial crisis and Covid. This cohort need jobs, just as literary departments need it to reinvigorate the discipline's perspectives and energies. But university administrators have to be persuaded about the value of literary criticism, purposes, properties, procedures, as a 'form of knowledge' in the way other disciplines exert their leverage in the academic market. So here's the intersection of literary methodology and employment tactics.

Making particularly good use of the neo-Aristotelian Alasdair MacIntyre's version of 'practice', Kramnick sets about anatomising the 'epistemic infrastructure' of literary analysis in its sequential three stages: 'close reading to contextual elaboration to argumentative synthesis'. But the 'form of knowledge' formula points in two directions. It's a way of doing the job, a discipline's distinctive techniques, skills, criteria, terminologies. It's also a question of the categories of knowledge, the sorts of truths, that a discipline claims to be producing. We might perhaps know how zoology or history exemplifies such categories, but it might be harder to demonstrate – especially to a sceptical university administrator – how criticism of poetry or the novel can be taxonomized, methodologically and conceptually, and exactly what sort of knowledge is being generated. This is the minefield that Kramnick treads warily, avoiding the reduction of the discipline's complexities to some paradigm's tidy protocols.

The core of his account – a defence of literary criticism as a discipline as more than a bricolage of *ad hoc* imaginative manoeuvres – is offered as the sequence of 'close reading as method, method as skilled practice, practice as creative action, and creative action as justified truth'. Much of his account unpacks that rolling rhetoric through ruminations on worked examples, teasing out an infrastructure. But the openness remains: on a Monday, criticism might claim to reveal the meaning of the poem and how that meaning is embodied, though for the rest of the week it might be more cautiously seen as part of a conversation about the complex, polyvalent cultural product. Kramnick doffs his cap where you'd expect: Guillory and Gadamer, Popper and Polyani, MacIntyre and Toril Moi, Ryle and the Russian Formalists, along with a pantheon from the *PMLA,* referenced for compass bearing and caveats. The practice emerges as a *praxis* with problematic shifts from close analysis of texture in a quotation (why this one rather than some differing other?) to an account of an overall structure; from micro- to macro-interpretation, and the hermeneutic circle of that shift. Kramnick examines the source of verification that might be adduced for the sorts of truth that might be claimed (is it 'falsifiable' *pace* Popper?) while cheerfully dropping in his hypothesis that literary criticism is itself a 'sort of creative writing'. Moreover, he argues that the close reading that goes on in the classroom might be more of a base line, the key note of the whole enterprise, than the subsequent published prod-

uct in the learned articles' expositions and systematising theoretics.

But constructing an authority for literary criticism goes beyond its mechanics and helping young academics squeeze into the market. The final chapter reaches out to 'public criticism for a public humanities'. Literary criticism has to define and hold its place in 'the value of the humanities for social flourishing and of criticism for understanding the world'. Matthew Arnold beckons? A world outside the text? Post-structuralists shudder. No truck here with self-referential literary chatter. Yet it isn't all a war zone: Kramnick allows an element of 'celebration of academic practice and academic life'. His discourse on method isn't Cartesian: he doesn't advocate new principles or procedures, but more modestly works to define what the insurance companies call the terms and conditions of the contract, though in a framework that must accommodate 'torque and spin'. It's a framework that would have been readily enough recognised in the years of, say, Leavis and Empson – who, as it happens, had their own problems in getting their university posts – but this is an erudite, closely argued and engaging essay, even something of a tract for the times, though whether it might exert any 'torque and spin' in the jobs freeze seems a stretch.

# What Tuned It Wrong

Declan Ryan, *Crisis Actor* (Faber) £10.99

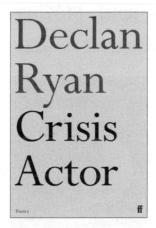

Reviewed by Hilary Menos

In *Crisis Actor*, Declan Ryan's poetic landscape, if not his actual emotional landscape, is dominated by men – as either macho heroes or lost souls. There are boxers – Joe Louis, Muhammad Ali, Diego Corrales and Mike Tyson to name just four, plus a quote at the front from Sonny Liston. Ryan also name-checks a cohort of older male poets associated with Colin Falck's Thurlow Road poetry workshop: the title poem, for example, is *in memoriam* Ian Hamilton, another is titled 'Colin Falck', another is

dedicated to Hugo Williams. And there are poems about singer-songwriter Nick Drake, soul legend Sam Cooke, Irish politician Charles Stewart Parnell, as well as a father, and a musician friend '– our beautiful boy'.

Women, however, rarely swim into focus and are generally not named. Of course this isn't necessarily a problem – only a fool would demand inclusivity and diversity in the subject index of a poetry collection. Art isn't about meeting targets or filling quotas (though it can be political, and it will have broader appeal if it draws from a plurality of voices). But for a female reader, parts of *Crisis Actor* can be a bit like one of those old movies where all the women play bit parts, whisky's the only drink taken, and nobody goes to the loo.

The boxing pieces, however, are glorious and vivid, active and human (most of his 2019 New Walk pamphlet *Fighters, Losers* is included). Ryan makes excellent use of 'found material', incorporating it into rangy, streetwise, busy poems. In 'Ethiopia Shall Stretch Forth Her Hands' (about a fight between Joe Louis and Primo Carnera), he lists Carnera's breakfast items: 'nineteen pieces of toast, fourteen eggs, / a loaf of bread and half a pound of Virginia ham'. In the fight,

[...] in the Yankee Stadium,
Carnera will sink to his knees
'slowly, like a great chimney that had been dynamited'.

Boxing, as a sport undertaken almost exclusively by poor working-class blokes, is inescapably political. Ryan's poetry also addresses poverty, class and emigration in Irish politics and history. His long (four-page) poem 'The Range' mourns the death of his maternal grandmother: 'You died at home, / light as a bird, bald as a young, blind bird'. The poem sets one woman's story of distress, poverty and medical neglect alongside a commentary on Irish history, and includes a version of the twelfth-century Irish poem 'Cumhthach Labhras an Lonsa':

*There is sadness in this blackbird's song,*
*and I know well what tuned it wrong.*

Ryan further explores the harshness of his own familial poverty in 'Fathers and Sons', where he waits for his father to come home from work – 'the patched up vest / hanging on for another month' – and narrates his father's evening: 'Hair washed in the kitchen sink [...] The absence of anything like pleasure'. In the book's opening poem, 'Sidney Road', Ryan positions himself somewhere between his Irish past and his London present. Gentrification has made Sidney Road, with its wisteria and identikit SUVs, into a place 'somewhere between coma and contentment' – one senses that Ryan feels both part of his new world and alienated from it.

These more recent poems feel more serious, better turned, but perhaps less engaging. Content and language come together beautifully, however, in some. In 'Rope-a-Dope' his own heart behind his ribs is an 'inmate: a pouting lifer'. And in 'Mayfly', describing a pub stop-off on the way home after a weekend country break, Ryan skilfully creates a tone of languid, wistful longing for a place where people 'live their whole lives, / most likely, / watch this cherry tree convulse intocwinter, what, / seventy times maybe'.

# Small Violently Moving Creature

V.R. 'Bunny' Lang, *The Miraculous Season: Selected Poems*, edited by Rosa Campbell (Carcanet) £16.99

Reviewed by Mae Losasso

It is a strange experience to hold the selected poems of a dead writer in your hand, turn to the introduction, and be told by the book's editor that 'you probably haven't heard of' the author. Of course, if we're holding the book, then we probably have heard of V.R. 'Bunny' Lang, but Rosa Campbell's apophatic introduction is a clever move, setting the scene for Lang's work in context. Because 'if you have [heard of Lang]', Campbell continues, 'it's because you're a Frank O'Hara fan and can recall poems dedicated to her'. Lang the friend; Lang the muse; Lang, one more name among the Joes, Janes and Jacksons of O'Hara's dazzling New York coterie. Such is the state of Lang reception; one always framed by the better-known O'Hara – and one that *The Miraculous Season* will no doubt help to redress.

But why open with O'Hara at all? Is it because Lang's poems need to lean on his, like a crutch, to be heard? In other words, does Lang's work require the New York School context to give it meaning? The answer, as the poems reveal, is mixed: on the one hand, Lang is significant as a woman in the first wave of the New York School (that rare bird that Campbell's critical work has, elsewhere, sought to bring into the light); on the other, her writing is at its best when it is least in the spirit of that School; or when it least resembles O'Hara's:

Spring you came marvellous with possibilities
Marvels sparked everywhere burning from bracken
Lichen crept crackling, and long grass

'The Pitch' opens with a typically O'Harian apostrophe to spring and its marvels; but it is the verbal textures that mark the poem out as a Lang composition. Like a spark catching on dry wood and bursting into flame, Lang follows the repeated sound of a click – 'sparked', 'bracken', 'lichen', 'crackling' – over an enjambed line, refusing end rhymes, but letting other alliterations build in synchrony ('burning from bracken'; 'lichen crept crackling'). Towards the end of the poem, these tongued textures reach virtuosic pitch; we can almost feel the weight of each word as it falls:

But in the fall the earth fell and I followed
Fell and dropped me into darkness like a death
Where I shut out and dull and dour and tacit

These are poems that repay a vocal reading. When it lands, Lang's play with the textures of words as they roll around and out of the mouth is unparalleled among her New York School contemporaries. There's an echo of Gerard Manley Hopkins in the thickly alliterative, enjambed lines; Auden (whom Lang loved) is audible; so is Dylan Thomas (as Campbell tells us, Lang 'hosted the first American reading by Dylan Thomas of *Under Milk Wood*'); and there are cadences that resemble the children's verse of Edward Lear ('Wicked secret crab') and Hilaire Belloc ('All the horses neighing *George*, children / Playing, saying, *George*').

Lang died at the age of thirty-two from Hodgkin's disease. Reading these poems, there's a frustration in knowing that this is a voice that couldn't meet its potential: flashes of brilliance do shine through, but there is something erratic about these moments, which dart and then fade, so that the spark never quite builds into the flame of a great poem. Or almost never. Little of the archival material on which Campbell drew was dated, so it's hard to trace a poetic development, but one senses something like the maturation of Lang's voice in 'Poems to Preserve the Years at Home', the long work that appears towards the end of the book, and which Campbell calls Lang's 'magnum opus':

Cocktail party. It takes all day to dress.
Thinking about it. Eat. Wash. Finally
The exquisite touches, employing Choice.
To this one I'll wear pale green silk stockings

They'll [sic] be nothing but poets there. Or the writers
Of terse short stories. One celebrity.
Catch as can can. A green silk handkerchief too.

This is Miss Lang, Miss V.R. Lang. The Poet, or
The Poetess...              Bynum, would you introduce
Someone else as         this is J.P. Hatchet
Who is a Roman Catholic?         No. Then don't do
That to me again. It's not an employment,
It's a private religion. Who's that over there?

This feels more familiarly like a New York School poem, Lang sounding the note of louche ennui that characterises O'Hara's best work. We are pulled into the orbit of Lang's bored anticipation. We can see – almost *feel* – the 'green silk stockings', those 'exquisite touches' that make the poem palpable. Texturally, there's a sense of Lang pulling on the reins: she's slowed her often breathless voice, suppressing her metrical bounce – but here and there she lets it bubble to the surface: 'Catch as can can'. This tonal restraint is echoed in the pageantry of social etiquette: among 'terse short stor[y]' writers, the dramatized 'Miss V.R. Lang. Poet' buttons up her 'strong, opinionated, passionate' self (these are all words, Campbell tells us, used by Lang's friends to describe her) – but not for long:

Spent late last night with stinking brigands
Who capered through my sleep like dirty clowns

[...]

My promises squeak and sneak,
Like dreaming burglars scheming in their sleep.

Trying to trace aesthetic connections between the disparate members of the New York School can feel like an arcane task, but in lines like these, Lang seems to be the missing piece. There are traces of early O'Hara, but there's also an Ashberyan weirdness, a Guestian cadence, even a Kochian comedy. And above all, there's *Lang*. When we come to know her voice, when we learn its distinctive strangeness, then the crutch of O'Hara falls quietly away and 'the small violently moving creature, here, / Is myself'.

# Ready for Your Close-Up?

Kathryn Gray, *Hollywood or Home* (Seren) £9.99; Dawn Watson, *We Play Here* (Granta) £10.99

Granta Poetry

Reviewed by Sarah-Clare Conlon

Showcasing forty-five poems themed around celebrity, Kathryn Gray's 'long-awaited second collection' (Nick Laird's blurb) isn't quite on the LA-born 'unretirement' tip – Gray being busy with various projects including as co-gatekeeper of the online journal *Bad Lilies.* As the poet herself acknowledges, though, it's been a while – 'Fresh Hell' admits: 'I have a book out. My book has been out for sixteen years. Sixteen long years.'

It's now an even longer stretch since her 2004 debut, *The Never-Never,* though Gray's though Gray's nine-poem pamphlet, *Flowers*, did make a cameo appearance in 2017. That appears in its entirety in *Hollywood or Home*, including *The Deer Hunter* tribute 'A Bandana', the mid-eighties-all-American-coming-of-age-movie-inspired trip-tych 'Shermerverse', and 'Testament', a kind of angst-ridden teenage love ballad to that book title's Mr Flowers, lead singer of The Killers: 'O Brandon, my brown-eyed boy, I will not answer / critics who say you're a triumph of style over substance...'

There's a nod therein to Googling ('hourly'), and there is much in *Hollywood or Home* requiring research or prior knowledge. Modern movie parlance should allow most readers 'The Meet-Cute' – a well-rounded piece that invites complicity with the reader – or phrases such as 'But here comes the money shot. We fade to black' in the midpoint poem 'High Concept'. Nods to specifics, however, and references to perhaps less familiar famous faces than, say, Meryl Streep, and my poor little smart-phone was melting. After a full forty-five entries, each needing some level of explanation, and with the 'Notes to the poems' section more questions than answers, I felt a little lie-down in my trailer coming on. Perhaps I'm just more home than Hollywood.

Combined with a lot of italics, kind of eyebrow-raised asides, and a total of forty-five screamers – equating to an average of one exclamation mark per poem! – a thought crept in that I was actually perhaps the uncool kid who's always laughing but never quite gets the in-jokes. Maybe I missed something. Perhaps the super-conversational tone – 'So I "loved" some guy in an alley in Rome' ('Durante'); 'So I was getting an enema somewhere off Ventura...' ('As told by Alan Smithee') – is a conversation I'm just not part of.

Still, there is much to admire in this collection – maybe it's simply that the less glitzy offerings tend to suffer bleach-out in the lightbulb glare of the real atten-tion-seekers such as 'Donald' (fifty-three lines, each starting with the first name of the forty-fifth president of the US; shudder) and the Johnny Cash number 'The Cave'. 'Cold Open', for instance, gives a shutter-quick but grounding glimpse into a personal world beyond celebrity and celluloid: 'at least believing yourself to be believing / yourself to be writing yourself down'. 'KCN' (the chemical formula of potassium cyanide), mean-while, is a chilling, accomplished and meaningful take on a particular incident in the aftermath of the Cro-at-Bosniak war. 'Away with the Birds', with its imagery and assonance, slows down the pace to consider that one man's madness is another man's sanity; 'Holly-wood', with its 'I have never anaphora', aligns the reader with the poet as both being mere witnesses to this glam-orous but glib other-world. Even the intriguingly gappy 'Meta' and its look-at-me cover-star yellow dress (yes of *La La Land*, but also of all the other dresses that feature – hick, red, blue, new) ends up as just another photo-bomber.

Belfast-born Dawn Watson has given herself an uphill task with *We Play Here*: a long poem told by four separate voices, all similar and all relating their own version of the same story, set in the gritty north of the city during the Troubles. She wrote it during Lockdown; perhaps confinement helped.

Each of the four sections' narrators is a strong story-teller and their chatty style cracks along the pace. We have Nell, the tomboy and self-proclaimed Queen of the Sticklebacks, who imagines water everywhere; Max, the wannabe poisoner (Brasso her weapon of choice, which is funny given her love of metal music); Sam, the superstitious sleuth who counts everything and gets the family groceries on tick; and Ellen, the thoughtful one, whose favourite film is *Stand by Me*, and whose thoughts seem older than her years ('The clouds were heavy on top of the twin yellow cranes').

Content warning: violence, domestic and otherwise, looms large, be it forced evictions and homes threatened with demolition, flood and fire, gossip of suicides, disappearances and kids crushed by piles of sand, soldiers and Saracens on the streets, Windowlened glass at Max's house ('Her dad is important and scares people').

Dialect (for Emma's, 'You say it Amma's') and slang (guddies, snib, taigs, youse) create authenticity, as do interesting turns of phrase: 'sallied out'; 'hoofed away'. Everyone has nicknames – Lonely Luke, Wee Jim, Blue and Red, Hatchet Man – and cultural references pin the reader in the summer of 1988. There are Curly Wurlys, Star Bars and Blue Riband biscuits ('which were the nicest'), cans of Harp, Stryke and Guinness, Crazy Prices and Primark, MFI wardrobes and Ford Cortinas.

There are also lots of rich images and textured language – street lights fizz and telephone wires fritz, thinks Max, while the TV masts on Divis mountain are 'like an Ulster Golgotha'; Sam muses that: 'Red metal washing poles in rows, no clothes on them. / They stand rusty, out of place, like trees on the moon.'

As well as the quartet of eleven- and twelve-year-old girls – 'It was a month until big school started' – the book has no end of characters, which leans it prosewards (indeed the Acknowledgements nod to some of the writing having previously appeared in short fiction anthologies). There are housing estate bullies and helpful shopkeepers, local bogeymen and women waiting for buses into town asking after each other's safety.

This is poetry as storytelling, and it's quite a story to tell. The scenes laid out and situations served up stick with you even once the book is neatly stowed on the shelf, and I found myself pondering what became of this gang of girls, what became of all these people in this community, much as you might with a short story or novel. I might even read it again.

# Some Contributors

**Gregory Woods**'s most recent collection was *Records of an Incitement to Silence* (Carcanet, 2021). His new booklet, *They Exchange Glances: Gay Modernist Poems in Translation*, is published by Hercules Editions.

**Sarah-Clare Conlon** has published a prose chapbook, *Marine Drive* (Broken Sleep Books), and three poetry pamphlets: *cache-cache* (Contraband Books), *Using Language* (Invisible Hand Press) and *Lune* (Red Ceilings Press), a Poetry Book Society Winter 2023 selection.

**Hilary Menos** won the Forward Prize for Best First Collection 2010 with *Berg* (Seren, 2009). She read PPE at Oxford, took an MA in poetry at MMU, and is editor of The Friday Poem.

**Gwyneth Lewis** wrote the inscription on the front of the Wales Millennium Centre and was National Poet of Wales. Her third memoir, *Nightshade Mother: A Disentangling*, about emotional abuse, is forthcoming. Gwyneth teaches at Middlebury College's Bread Loaf School of English and has recently been Artist in Residence at Balliol College, Oxford.

**Mae Losasso** is a Leverhulme Early Career Fellow at the University of Warwick. Her first book, *Poetry, Architecture, and the New York School: Something Like a Liveable Space* was published by Palgrave Macmillan in 2023.

**Mike Freeman** was a lecturer at Manchester, a factotum at Carcanet, now a Pennine montagnard.

**Galina Rymbu** was born in 1990 in the city of Omsk (Siberia, Russia) and lives in Lviv, Ukraine. She edits *F-Pis'mo*, an online magazine for feminist literature and theory, as well as Gryoza, a website for contemporary poetry. *Life in Space*, her first collection in English translation, was published in 2020 by UDP.

**Sasha Dugdale**'s sixth book of poems, *The Strongbox*, is published in May 2024.

**Anthony V. Capildeo** is a Professor at the University of York. New work includes *Polkadot Wounds* (Carcanet, 2024), inspired by the Charles Causley Trust, and a collaboration with Mike Chin and Hope Mohr.

**Stanley Moss**, major American poet, just published his *Goddamned Selected Poems* with Carcanet. He has eighteen poetry books that fight for the lyrical truth with original weapons. He makes the ordinary beautiful and extraordinary.

Earlier this year New Zealander **Gregory O'Brien** accompanied his exhibition of art and poetry, 'From an island in the antipodes', to England (or Ingarani, in Maori), where it was shown at the Manchester Poetry Library.

**Éireann Lorsung** works and teaches in a field of images, objects movement, and texts. Her most recent collection is *The Century* (Milkweed Editions).

**John Gallas** is an Aotearoa/NZ poet and the author of thirty-three books, as well as a translator and librettist.

**Kirsty Gunn** has a new collection of short stories coming out this year, *Pretty Ugly*.

**Alex Stanley** was born and raised in Arizona. He earned a BA in English from Boston College and an MFA in Creative Writing at the University of California, Irvine.

**Hal Coase** is a poet and playwright. His poetry has been published in *The White Review* and anthologised by Carcanet (2020) and Prototype (2023). He lives in Rome.

---

*Editors*
Michael Schmidt
John McAuliffe

*Editorial Manager*
Andrew Latimer

*Contributing Editors*
Anthony Vahni Capildeo
Sasha Dugdale
Will Harris

*Copyeditor*
Maren Meinhardt

*Designed by*
Andrew Latimer

*Editorial address*
The Editors at the address on the right. Manuscripts cannot be returned unless accompanied by a stamped addressed envelope or international reply coupon.

*Trade distributors*
Combined Book Services Ltd

*Represented by*
Compass IPS Ltd

*Copyright*
© 2024 Poetry Nation Review
All rights reserved
ISBN 978-1-80017-420-7
ISBN 0144-7076

*Subscriptions—6 issues*
INDIVIDUAL–print and digital:
£45; abroad £65
INSTITUTIONS–print only:
£76; abroad £90
INSTITUTIONS–digital only:
from Exact Editions (https://shop.exacteditions.com/gb/pn-review)
to: PN Review, Alliance House, 30 Cross Street, Manchester, M2 7AQ, UK.

*Supported by*

Supported using public funding by
ARTS COUNCIL ENGLAND